Shouting Won't Grow Dendrites

Second Edition

Shouting Won't Grow Dendrites

Second Edition

20 Techniques to Detour Around the Danger Zones

Marcia L. Tate

CORWIN
A SAGE Company

CORWIN
A SAGE Company

FOR INFORMATION:

Corwin
A SAGE Company
2455 Teller Road
Thousand Oaks, California 91320
(800) 233-9936
www.corwin.com

SAGE Publications Ltd.
1 Oliver's Yard
55 City Road
London EC1Y 1SP
United Kingdom

SAGE Publications India Pvt. Ltd.
B 1/I 1 Mohan Cooperative Industrial Area
Mathura Road, New Delhi 110 044
India

SAGE Publications Asia-Pacific Pte. Ltd.
3 Church Street
#10-04 Samsung Hub
Singapore 049483

Printed in the United States of America.

A catalog record of this book is available from the Library of Congress.

ISBN 978-1-4833-5097-4

Acquisitions Editor: Jessica Allan
Associate Editor: Kimberly Greenberg
Editorial Assistant: Cesar Reyes
Project Editor: Veronica Stapleton Hooper
Copy Editor: Pam Schroeder
Typesetter: C&M Digitals (P) Ltd.
Proofreader: Sarah J. Duffy
Indexer: Julie Grayson
Cover Designer: Michael Dubowe
Marketing Manager: Stephanie Trkay

This book is printed on acid-free paper.

SUSTAINABLE FORESTRY INITIATIVE
Certified Chain of Custody
At Least 10% Certified Forest Content
www.sfiprogram.org
SFI-01028

18 19 20 21 8 7 6 5 4 3

Contents

DETOUR ▶

DETOUR

Acknowledgments

In every school I visit, there are teachers whose classrooms are very effectively managed and whose students excel at extremely high levels. What's more impressive is that those teachers accomplish this amazing feat without ever raising their voices. You see, they have already figured out that Shouting Won't Grow Dendrites. This book is dedicated to that group of teachers because the proactive management skills that they have already mastered will be reflected in the chapters that follow.

This book is also dedicated to those teachers who are striving daily to become better at what they do, for to be dissatisfied with the status quo is to strive toward perfection. I pray that this book enables them to realize that the best-run classrooms are positive places to be, where teachers present challenging, activity-based lessons and where students believe that, academically, all things are possible.

I also dedicate this book to my parents, Alvin and Eurica, who instilled in me and my two sisters the values and respect that are lacking in growing numbers of today's students. I will be forever grateful for the times we said, *"No sir,"* to my father and, *"Yes ma'am,"* to my mother. Their highest of expectations equipped us with the confidence, skills, and abilities to be successful at whatever we undertook. Tyrone and I have attempted to do the same with our three children—Jennifer, Jessica, and Christopher—and our four grandchildren—Christian, Aidan, Maxwell, and Aaron.

To my husband, Tyrone: For more than 35 years, you have been my confidant and best friend. Thank you for your continued love and encouragement, which enable me to perform at my best during every presentation.

Thanks to the associates who work with our company, Developing Minds, Inc. You are instrumental in spreading the word that all students can succeed. I am also grateful to Carol Purviance and Fran Rodrigues, our administrative assistants, who *keep me straight* both professionally and personally and ensure that the company runs smoothly on a daily basis.

About the Author

 **Marcia L. Tate, EdD,** is the former executive director of professional development for the DeKalb County School System, Decatur, Georgia. During her 30-year career with the district, she has been a classroom teacher, reading specialist, language arts coordinator, and staff development executive director. She received the Distinguished Staff Development Award for the state of Georgia, and her department was chosen to receive the Exemplary Program Award for the state.

Marcia is currently an educational consultant and has taught more than 400,000 parents, teachers, administrators, and business and community leaders throughout the world, including Australia, Egypt, Greece, Hungary, Oman, Singapore, Thailand, and New Zealand. She is the author of the following six best sellers: *Worksheets Don't Grow Dendrites: 20 Instructional Strategies That Engage the Brain* (2nd Ed.); *"Sit & Get" Won't Grow Dendrites: 20 Professional Learning Strategies That Engage the Adult Brain* (2nd Ed.); *Reading and Language Arts Worksheets Don't Grow Dendrites: 20 Literacy Strategies That Engage the Brain* (2nd Ed.); *Shouting Won't Grow Dendrites: 20 Techniques for Managing a Brain-Compatible Classroom* (2nd Ed.); *Mathematics Worksheets Don't Grow Dendrites: 20 Numeracy Strategies That Engage the Brain*, and her book for parents, *Preparing Children for Success in School and in Life: 20 Ways to Increase Your Child's Brain Power.* Her most recent books are *Science Worksheets Don't Grow Dendrites: 20 Instructional Strategies That Engage the Brain*, cowritten with Warren Phillips, and *Social Studies Worksheets Don't Grow Dendrites: 20 Instructional Strategies That Engage the Brain.* Participants in her workshops refer to them as *some of the best they have ever experienced* since Marcia uses the 20 brain-compatible strategies outlined in her books to actively engage her audiences.

Marcia received her bachelor's degree in psychology and elementary education from Spelman College in Atlanta, Georgia. She earned her master's degree in remedial reading from the University of Michigan, her specialist degree in educational leadership from Georgia State University, and her doctorate in educational leadership from Clark Atlanta University. Spelman College awarded her the Apple Award for excellence in the field of education.

Marcia is married to Tyrone Tate and is the proud mother of three children—Jennifer, Jessica, and Christopher—and the doting grand-mother of four grandchildren—Christian, Aidan, Maxwell, and Aaron. Tyrone and Marcia own the consulting firm Developing Minds Inc. and can be contacted by calling (770) 918-5039 or by e-mail: marciata@bell south.net. Visit her website at www.developingmindsinc.com.

Introduction

If you have been in education for any length of time, you have probably observed one or both of the following scenarios. If not, attempt to visualize them as you read the paragraphs that follow.

➡ **SCENARIO I**

Mrs. Stephens teaches French at Fairmont High School. As her third-period students file into the room, she is sitting at her desk grading papers. She never looks up or acknowledges them until a group of students comes in playfully pushing and shoving one another. She yells at them from her seated position to calm down and sit down! They ignore her request. Once the bell rings, she stands and attempts to gain enough order to begin class. She has to wait several minutes until a majority of students stop talking to one another and laughing out loud. She then calls the roll, which takes several minutes because she calls the students by last name and waits for them to state that they are present. By this time, 8 minutes of the class period has passed. She then tells students to open their textbooks to page 67 and to get out their homework assignment from the previous night. Only a handful of students actually have the assignment, so the rest have nothing to look at as she goes over the answers. Once the homework assignment is checked, students take turns translating several passages contained in the French textbook into English. Mrs. Stephens stops periodically to scream at students who don't appear to be paying a bit of attention to the passage.

Mrs. Stephens then instructs students to get out paper and pencil because she will be lecturing on French culture and they will need to take notes. Several students have no paper and pencil, so she throws a tirade about the foibles of coming to class unprepared. She reminds them that it is their responsibility to bring the proper supplies. After all, she is fulfilling her obligation by teaching the material. It is not her fault if students choose not to learn it.

The walls in the room are bare. Except for a couple of purchased posters, there is nothing for students to look at daily as they learn French. Students are sitting in straight rows and are rarely allowed to talk with one another

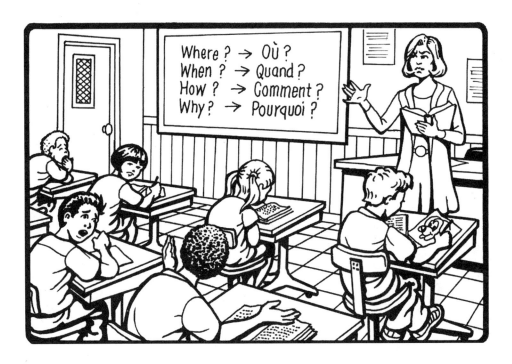

about what they are learning. In fact, Mrs. Stephens still considers it a good day if she is doing all the talking in class and the students are sitting quietly. It doesn't matter if they are not paying any attention to what she is saying, as long as they are quiet.

After what to students seems like an eternity, the bell rings, and every student jumps up from his or her desk and bounds out of the door. Mrs. Stephens has never moved from her desk, however, during the entire period.

SCENARIO II ⬅

Mr. Hernandez teaches Spanish at Longview High School. He is the favorite teacher of the majority of students who are fortunate enough to have him as their teacher. The bell has just rung, so you will find him standing at the door to bid farewell to the students who are leaving third period and hello to the ones who are entering for fourth. He can be overheard asking specific students if they won their football game played during the previous weekend and complimenting others on their appearance. You hear salsa music playing softly from a speaker in the room. Students have been taught from day one of school to talk beneath the music and not over it. That is not all they were taught. During the first few weeks of school, Mr. Hernandez spent more time teaching class routines and procedures than teaching Spanish. What was the benefit? He will spend the remainder of the year teaching more Spanish than routines and procedures.

If you look around Mr. Hernandez's classroom, it will look more like someone's home than a room in a high school. Students sit at tables where they work with peers, called family members. In the back of the room is a sofa. The fluorescent lights in the ceiling of the room have been turned off.

The lighting provided is a combination of natural light from the windows on one side of the room and low lamp lighting on the other side. As none of Mr. Hernandez's students have allergies, there is a distinct smell of vanilla in the classroom that has a calming effect on the brains of students. There is a word wall of Spanish vocabulary on one wall along with some pieces of artwork. On Mr. Hernandez's desk are pictures of his wife, children, and dogs. On the wall beside his desk are his degrees. There are some live plants adorning the room.

It took a while, but Mr. Hernandez has managed to develop a relationship with each of his students. He started with the ones that he thought probably needed him most. He gives students the confidence to believe that they can learn Spanish and uses brain-compatible strategies daily to engage the brains of his students. Learning in his class is challenging but so much fun! Today, they are participating in a role play of a real-life scenario of a typical day in the life of a teenager. The role play is presented in Spanish.

➡ BAD NEWS

Visualize yourself as a teacher in a one-room schoolhouse in the 1800s. A student has aggravated you for the fifth time in the same day! You have had enough, so you pull a revolver concealed under your jacket and demand that the student sit down immediately or be buried in the schoolyard. The student promptly sits down.

Fast-forward to the 2000s. A student has aggravated you for the fifth time in one day. You have had enough and request that the student sit down or be sent to the principal's office. The student curses you, laughs, and continues his or her mischief.

What a difference between the two scenarios, and neither one is acceptable! Even in the 1960s, the major disciplinary offenses involved talking too much in class, chewing gum, passing notes, or being out of a seat. Today, teachers are dealing with students' inability to pay attention, refusal to complete assigned work, blatant disrespect, and violence against them and their students. In fact, it is now the students who are concealing the weapons.

Here is the bad news! There are societal reasons why some of today's students can be more challenging to teach and to manage than ever before. By understanding the issues surrounding why some students act the way they do, educators are better able to understand the behaviors manifested in many classrooms. Let's examine eight of those issues and their effects on student behavior.

Lack of Attunement

The brain stands its best chance of growing normally if it is nurtured. From the moment a child is born, the parents or other caregivers should be in the child's face interacting with him or her. In fact, only one-fourth of children's brains are developed at birth. From birth on, each time a baby is held, fed, talked to, played with, sung to, or read to, the additional 75% develops. According to Eric Jensen (2009), this process, referred to as attunement, is most crucial during the first 6 to 24 months of life and enables babies to develop healthy emotions such as gratefulness, forgiveness, and empathy.

Many children in our schools have had no attunement. No one has talked to them, played with them, or interacted with them on a consistent basis. Of my three children, one, my son Christopher, suffered from lack of attunement. Chris is adopted, and we did not adopt him until he was almost a year old. For the first year of his life, he was in a foster home with an older foster mother who fed him and changed his diaper but interacted with him only on a limited basis. As a result, there were language delays.

Lack of Rocking, Holding, and Cherishing

Some children who have not been rocked, held, kissed, cherished, and told they matter to someone can literally grow up without empathy and sympathy for others. In a study of more than 10,000 infants admitted to Irish foundling homes in the 1900s, only 45 survived. The ironic thing is that the high mortality rate had little to do with nutritional deficits. Due to the lack of maternal nurturing over a 25-year period, the majority of those who survived grew up to be pathologically unstable (Joseph, 1999).

Examine the history of any serial killer. They were typically either verbally or physically abused usually prior to the age of 8. It is before this age that the brain develops empathy and sympathy for others. If children have not been shown any, they tend not to develop any.

Consider this analogy. What happens to pit bulls and other types of dogs who are groomed to fight other dogs? They are both verbally and physically abused by their caregivers, the people they trust. The dogs become so angry that they will fight to the death. Why do we think that it is any different for a human being? Children come to us angry and oppositional, and some of those feelings just may come from a lack of nurturing in the home.

Changing Family Structure

The structural makeup of the family is changing. There are single-parent families. There are grandparents raising children. There are aunts, uncles, cousins, and other family members raising children. There are children raising themselves. There are even two-parent families where the parents must spend so much time working to provide for their children's basic needs that they do not have adequate time to spend with their children. The average number of minutes that fathers spend in meaningful conversation with their children is 7 minutes per day. It is not much better for mothers at 11 minutes per day. If you spend more time than that with your children, take your dominant hand, reach across your body, and pat yourself on the back.

When you consider where that conversation used to take place, you will no doubt recall the dinner table. Many families do not eat dinner together anymore. Even when they are sitting together for a meal, that does not mean they are actually talking. My husband, Tyrone, and I were eating dinner in a restaurant in Atlanta. I was observing a family of four sitting close by—a mother, father, and two teenage sons. In more than an hour, they never said one word to one another. One of the sons had earbuds in his ears and was listening to music on his iPod. The second son could not eat for texting on his iPhone. The father was reading *USA Today*, and the mother was staring into space. I turned to Ty and commented on how the parents had just missed an hour-long opportunity to engage in meaningful conversation with their teenage sons. People wonder why so many teenagers are on the Internet forming relationships with strangers. There is no substitute for the strong relationships created when families spend quality time together.

Lack of Play

Stop right now, and visualize when you were little. If you are in my age range or perhaps a bit younger, you will no doubt remember playing outdoors in the neighborhood with your friends. In the imagination you were developing, you were someone other than yourself! Your friends were also other people. The tree was your house, and you managed to find things in your environment that you could turn into other things. Little did you realize that this play helped your brain become creative. It also helped you to develop the social skills necessary to be able to share your toys and decide what you and your friends would do next.

Now, the majority of play is technological. While there can be benefits to this type of recreation, there are also some drawbacks. Why do children have to be creative and imaginative when many of the toys they play with provide visuals, in vivid, living color, no less? Oftentimes, children are playing beside one another as they activate their joysticks rather than with one another.

A few months ago, I witnessed this scenario. A 4-year-old in the creative play center of his preschool was supposed to be building a structure out of some large, flat building blocks. Rather than using the blocks to form a structure, he took one of the blocks, put it to his ear and pretended to be talking on what now had become his cell phone. I am sure he was imitating what he had seen the adults in his home do many times. When redirected to build something from the blocks, he related that he didn't know how.

Nutritional Deficits, Sedentary Lifestyle, and Lack of Sleep

This generation of children may be the first generation in 200 years whose life expectancy may be shorter than that of their parents (Colbert, 2009). Why? One of the reasons may be the inability of parents to feed their children foods that are healthy for their brains and bodies. As the Sonic and MacDonald's generation, many students have developed unhealthy eating habits.

There have always been people who were not healthy eaters. The major difference between then and now, however, is the fact that people in the past were working unhealthy foods off through manual labor jobs. The second reason for the shortened life expectancy is lack of movement. Children today have developed sedentary lifestyles as they sit in front of television, computers, video games, and so forth. This is one of the reasons that the Play60 initiative of the National Football League emphasizes eating healthy and 60 minutes of physical activity for each child daily.

Sleep is also crucial for healthy brain and body development. Many students come to class tired because they simply did not get enough sleep the previous night. Sleep serves three purposes. First, when a person is sleeping, the body is healing itself. For this reason, people with traumatic injuries are placed in induced comas so that they can sleep for long periods of time while the body repairs itself. Second, much of what a student learns during the day is processed at night when the brain is less active. If students do not get enough sleep, they can lose a lot of what is being taught during the day. Adults would do well to get 7 to 9 hours of sleep per night. Teenagers need more sleep than adults, so parents should be encouraged to put their children to bed in a timely fashion. Third, there appears to be a positive correlation between adequate sleep and weight loss. When the body is in a state of rest, hormones stand a better chance of being balanced. When hormones are balanced, it becomes much easier to lose weight.

Rapidly Changing Stimuli

Do you become impatient if your computer does not do what you need it to do the minute you push a designated key? Most people's patience for electronics, and everything else, is incredibly short. Thanks to advances in modern technology, we are used to things happening faster and faster—so much so that we don't feel the need to wait. I am as guilty as anyone. I can remember when I used to buy Jiffy Pop popcorn and wait 15 or more minutes to enjoy a delicious bowl of freshly popped corn. I would even have to shake the pan to keep it from burning. Now, I have a difficult time standing at the microwave waiting 2 to 3 minutes for my popcorn. We want what we want, and we want it now!

"I raised my hand and asked if I could leave
the room, and here I am."

Don't be surprised if your students appear restless or inattentive if your lecture goes on for far too long. Research relates that the average attention span of the brain is approximately equal to the age of the student. This would make the attention span of a 7-year-old 7 minutes, a 12-year-old 12 minutes, and a 16-year-old 16 minutes. Here is some more bad news! The attention span of an 80-year-old is not 80 minutes. The average attention span of the adult brain is approximately 20 minutes and getting shorter every day.

Increased Violence and Negativity in the Media

If it bleeds, it leads! Journalists and television producers know that the highest ratings are often derived from the most horrific news stories. As a result, the more positive fare is relegated to the back pages of the paper or not mentioned at all. When I was a child, the most violent shows were shown late at night. But, of course, violence in the 1950s and 1960s was getting shot on *Bonanza*. By the way, have you ever noticed that no matter where you were shot on *Bonanza*, at the end of the show, your arm was in a sling?

Now, at any time of the day or night, television is filled with shows that should not be seen by children. In fact, the American Academy of Pediatrics recommends that children under the age of 2 not watch television at all. After 2, parents should carefully select what shows the child will view. Many parents today, however, use television as a babysitter. Children are watching whatever they want to watch whenever they want to watch it.

While violence and profanity in music does not appear to negatively impact most normal brains (Feinstein, 2009), violence and negativity in music with visual components do. As children view more and more violence, the brain becomes immune to the shock value, and creators of videos know that they have to keep increasing the levels of violence to get the same response.

Increased Drug and Alcohol Use

When I am talking to high school students, I love to show them two distinct visuals—one of a normal, healthy brain and one of a brain after years of marijuana use. The latter brain looks misshapen and atrophied. Illegal drugs have always been with us. That is not news. What is news, however, is the number of people who are now abusing prescription drugs. In a recent article in *People* magazine, it is stated that deaths from prescription drugs now exceed the number of people killed in car crashes annually.

Drugs, whether prescription or not, alcohol, and nicotine from the cigarettes that many teenagers smoke are all potentially toxic for the body (Markowitz & Jensen, 2007). Contrary to popular belief, alcohol is a drug. Studies have shown that the brains of people who are heavy drinkers tend to weigh less, and the frontal lobes of their brains contain smaller and fewer memory cells, or neurons, than do those of nondrinkers (Markowitz & Jensen, 2007).

GOOD NEWS: PROACTIVE PLANNING ⬅

I try not to bring people bad news without also bringing them good news! The good news is that, even in the 21st century, with all the societal challenges that students have to face, there are exceptional classroom managers. The research tells us that effective managers do not necessarily possess this magic bag of tricks that other teachers do not. Instead, they have planned for their students in ways that keep classroom management problems from happening in the first place. In other words, they are proactive and not reactive.

Let's consider this real-world analogy to distinguish between the concepts of reactive and proactive planning. A highway runs right through the middle of a small town in Mexico. Unbeknownst to drivers, at the end of the highway, there is a drop-off that extends over a cliff. There are no signs that the cliff is coming up; therefore, before drivers can even put on their brakes, the cars fall off the cliff and end up in the valley below. The town council gets together to find a solution to the problem and decides to place an ambulance at the base of the cliff so that, when cars fall over, the driver and passengers can be rushed to the hospital in the shortest amount of time possible. This solution did not work! By the time some cars ended up in the valley below, an ambulance was unnecessary because the occupants of the car were already deceased. The town council reconvenes and makes a different decision. They decide to put up detour signs all along the highway to warn drivers about the cliff and detour them around the danger. Then, no car gets to the edge of the cliff in the first place.

This story is unbelievable, yet it is a metaphor for the difference between a reactive and a proactive classroom manager. Reactive or ineffective classroom managers wait until students get to the edge of the cliff or problems occur and then decide how they will deal with the situation. These teachers dole out disciplinary consequences depending on their mood or their feelings for a particular student, usually with a great deal of screaming, shouting, or other negative emotions. They appear annoyed, frustrated, and often engage students in power struggles, which teachers are always destined to lose. In many cases, the ambulance is waiting at the base of the cliff. The teacher puts the student in the ambulance and then sends the ambulance to after-school detention, in-school suspension, the principal's office, or home.

Proactive teachers do not wait until students get near the edge of the cliff because they are putting up detour signs in their classrooms to steer students around the potential danger.

Let us make this concept a little plainer. Have you ever noticed a group of middle or high school students who change classes, and in one teacher's class they are well behaved, but in another teacher's class they are terrors? Could it be that the former teacher has detour signs in place that the second teacher does not? The 20 chapters in this book are organized into five detour signs that every teacher should be putting up to help eliminate behavior problems before they even occur. Those detour signs are as follows:

- Get to know each student.
- Create a physical environment conducive to learning.
- Engage the brains of your students.
- Develop a proactive management plan.
- Deal proactively with challenging behavior.

Get to Know Each Student

Several years ago, I was observing in the classroom of a teacher who consistently experienced a large number of disciplinary offenses. Her students did not like her, and the feeling appeared to be mutual. The book bag of one of the students she liked was lying in the aisle near the student's desk. She politely asked the student to pick up the book bag and place it in the appropriate location so that she would not trip over it. The student complied. Several weeks later, I was once again observing the same teacher when a similar incident occurred. However, this particular book bag belonged to a student who happened to be one of her pet peeves. The reaction this time was totally different. She kicked the book bag while screaming at the student to get it out of her way. She even accused him of trying to trip her. The student shrugged his shoulders and reluctantly moved the bag while mumbling some indiscernible words under his breath. This student and teacher are destined for some future power struggles.

Chapters 1 through 3 will deal specifically with ways that teachers and students can develop relationships with one another. Without those relationships, the rest of the book is null and void. These chapters explain how to maintain high expectations for all students and understand the underlying causes behind why some students behave as they do.

Create a Physical Environment Conducive to Learning

Many behavior problems can be alleviated by the way a teacher sets up the physical environment in the classroom. Chapter 4 is devoted to creating a brain-compatible classroom that encourages the calming effect of natural or low light and discourages the use of fluorescent lighting, which can have detrimental effects on the health and well-being of both brain and body.

Teachers can actually change the state of the students' brains with the type of music they play. Chapter 5 will introduce the reader to the types of music that calm the brain down and place it in a state for learning. The number of beats in this music averages 50 to 70 per minute, which is the same as the heart. At other times, before students become lethargic, they need the uplifting, energetic tunes of a faster pace of music. Change their mood as you change the music!

Chapter 6 deals with the use of certain colors that can be used to calm or ignite creativity in the brains of students and even mentions *Irlen syndrome,* which is a condition that some people have that inhibits them from reading black print on white paper.

Aromatherapy is big business due to the impacts that specific smells can have on the brain. Although Chapter 7 will touch on this topic, teachers must be careful of the ill effects of certain aromas on those students who have allergies. Teachers may want to save the tips in this chapter for their homes, where they can best relieve the stresses of the school day.

Providing alternative seating such as tables and chairs, sofas, beanbag chairs, rockers, or carpet on the floor enables students to explore other options for seating rather than the most uncomfortable piece of furniture on the face of the earth—the student desk, which they are required to occupy for the majority of the day. Chapter 8 will provide additional research on ways to make the classroom feel more like home.

Engage the Brains of Your Students

Many instances of inappropriate behavior can be linked to students who are bored by the content or feel unable to accomplish the assigned tasks. They cover their boredom and inadequacy with misbehavior. A teacher's best line of defense against behavior problems is that teacher's ability to actively engage students in meaningful and relevant lessons. In five best-sellers of the *Worksheets Don't Grow Dendrites: 20 Instructional Strategies That Engage the Brain* series, I have identified 20 brain-compatible strategies that take advantage of the way the brain learns best.

Learning style theorists (Dewey, 1934; Gardner, 1983; Marzano, 2007; Sternberg & Grigorenko, 2000) and educational consultants (Jensen, 2008, 2009; Sousa, 2006, 2009; Willis, 2006, 2007) who research the brain agree that there are some instructional strategies that, by their very nature, take advantage of ways in which brains learn best. They should be used in every classroom, regardless of the content or the grade level, because they simply work for all brains—regular-education brains, special-education brains, gifted brains, English-as-a-second-language (ESL) brains, attention-deficit brains, and autistic brains. These strategies not only enable teachers to address both hemispheres of the brain, but they increase academic achievement for all students, they decrease behavior problems, and they make teaching and learning so much fun! Chapters 9 through 13 provide research regarding the use of the strategies for effective student engagement.

The 20 strategies are as follows:

1. Brainstorming and discussion

2. Drawing and artwork

3. Field trips

4. Games

5. Graphic organizers, semantic maps, and word webs

6. Humor

7. Manipulatives, experiments, labs, and models

8. Metaphors, analogies, and similes

9. Mnemonic devices

10. Movement

11. Music, rhythm, rhyme, and rap

12. Project-based and problem-based instruction

13. Reciprocal teaching and cooperative learning

14. Role plays, drama, pantomimes, and charades

15. Storytelling

16. Technology

17. Visualization and guided imagery

18. Visuals

19. Work study and apprenticeships

20. Writing and journals

Refer to the Comparison of Brain-Compatible Instructional Strategies to Learning Theory chart (Table 9.1) in Chapter 9 for a correlation of the 20 brain-compatible strategies to Howard Gardner's Theory of Multiple Intelligences and to the four major modalities—(1) visual, (2) auditory, (3) kinesthetic, and (4) tactile.

Develop a Proactive Management Plan

When I began teaching more than 40 years ago, my classroom management plan consisted of many rules, harsh consequences, and few rewards. Even today, some teachers are searching for the most severe consequences in an effort to squelch the inappropriate behaviors they are seeing daily in their classrooms. Here is the problem. The students who are the most challenging are often the ones who have had every consequence in the book thrown at them, and it has simply made little difference. If consequences are so effective, why do such a large percentage of convicted criminals reoffend within 3 years of their initial release from prison?

It appears to be the positive experiences between teacher and student that correlate to sustained improvements in student behavior. These experiences include a teaching of those rituals and procedures essential for effective functioning, celebrations for improved student performance, low-profile interventions when students are off task, and finally, appropriate consequences for more high-profile misbehavior. Chapters 14 through 18 are devoted to these topics.

Deal Proactively With Challenging Behavior

No matter how proactive a teacher is, there may be some chronic behavior problems for which one cannot prepare. Being proactive, in this case, means becoming informed about the brains of students who may learn or behave very differently from the norm and soliciting assistance from others when that help is warranted. Chapters 19 and 20 provide an overview of chronic behavior challenges such as attention deficit hyperactivity disorder (ADHD), conduct disorder, learned helplessness, oppositional defiant disorder (ODD), acute stress disorder, and depression.

Students who possess these different ways of behaving can be the greatest challenges for even the best teacher. However, the more a teacher understands the unique brains of these students, the more equipped the teacher is to formulate an arsenal of possible solutions to the puzzles these students provide.

The final chapter stresses the importance of maintaining a positive relationship with the parents of all of your students but especially the most challenging ones. A parent is a child's first and best teacher and can provide major insights into the causes and solutions of his or her child's behavior.

➡ OVERVIEW OF THE BOOK

This book is the second edition of the original text, *Shouting Won't Grow Dendrites*, and a part of the multiple content area series regarding brain-compatible instruction. The additional books in the series are as follows:

- *Worksheets Don't Grow Dendrites: 20 Instructional Strategies That Engage the Brain*, 2nd ed. (2010)
- *Reading and Language Arts Worksheets Don't Grow Dendrites: 20 Literacy Strategies That Engage the Brain*, 2nd ed. (2014)
- *Mathematics Worksheets Don't Grow Dendrites: 20 Numeracy Strategies That Engage the Brain, PreK–8* (2009)
- *Science Worksheets Don't Grow Dendrites: 20 Instructional Strategies That Engage the Brain* (2011)
- *Social Studies Worksheets Don't Grow Dendrites: 20 Instructional Strategies That Engage the Brain* (2012)

This book attempts to accomplish the following four major objectives:

1. Provide five *detour signs* that proactive teachers can use to direct students around the dangers of misbehavior

2. Review more than 200 pieces of updated research regarding why these practices are essential for managing a classroom where excellence abounds

3. Supply more than 200 classroom examples for implementing proactive management practices that effective teachers use

4. Provide time and space at the end of each chapter for the reader to reflect on the application of these practices as they apply them to their own personal classrooms

➡ SUMMARY

When teachers are reactive, rather than proactive, behavior problems may truly upset them because they have not anticipated the problems and are not equipped with possible solutions. This stress or frustration may result in increased use of sarcasm, random punishments, and even shouting or yelling. But *Shouting Won't Grow Dendrites*. In fact, consider this simile. It has been said that shouting to manage students is like blowing the horn to steer a car. After all, excessive blowing of horns escalates road rage just like excessive shouting at students escalates power struggles. In my observations, teachers who yell at students can have students who yell back, causing the teacher to yell even louder and the vicious cycle to continue.

Proactive classroom managers steer students around possible danger with the five detour signs delineated in this book. They develop relationships with all students; they arrange their classroom to create a calming state for learning; they engage the brains of all students with relevant, interactive lessons; they put in place a proactive management plan that provides structure for each day; and they get assistance with the most challenging students.

One band director in Alexandria, Louisiana, summed it up quite nicely. He related to me over lunch that there are three adjectives that describe his success in managing the band. He told me, *"I am the three Fs. I am firm, fair, and friendly."* I have added three more *Fs* to his. Proactive classroom managers are also *fun, flexible,* and *forgiving!*

DETOUR →

Get to Know Each Student

1

Develop a Relationship With Each Student

*If your students like you, there is nothing
they will not do <u>for</u> you.*

*If your students don't like you, there is nothing
they will not do <u>to</u> you!*

Marcia L. Tate

WHAT: CREATING A CARING CULTURE

Have you ever walked down the hall in a high school and seen a teenager with his pants hanging low and a cap on his head? Have you witnessed one teacher ask the student to pull up his pants and take off the cap, and he walks by as if he has not heard the teacher's request? Keep watching! The student continues to walk, and another teacher makes the same request. *"Pull up your pants and take off your cap!"* This time the student complies.

What made the difference? It was the relationship that the student had with the second teacher that he did not have with the first. Relationships are everything to classroom management.

Teachers have told me that their students don't really have to like them. It is only important that students respect them. Guess what! According to brain research, students must both like you and respect you! Think back to a teacher in your educational career that you did not like. No doubt, you will never forget the experience of being in his or her room. However, you will not remember much of the content he or she taught. As you were sitting in the room, your brain may have been in survival mode. This means that the higher-level thought processes of the brain may have given way to the fight-or-flight response that occurs when one is threatened.

If you have a relationship with students and they misbehave, they are truly sorry because they have disappointed you. If you have no relationship, they don't really care whether they disappoint you or not. I have seen blended families where the stepparent does not bother to develop a relationship with the stepchildren but begins to make demands on them. I have actually heard teenage stepchildren make this comment: "You can't tell me what to do. You are not my mother!" When time is spent developing that all-important relationship, then the teenager is more likely to comply when the stepparent asks them to be home from a date by midnight.

According to William Glasser (1999), one of the five crucial needs that must be satisfied if students are to be effectively motivated is the need for belonging and love. The other needs are survival, power, freedom, and fun. The need for belonging and love used to be satisfied for most students by belonging to a stable family unit. Many children today have no strong family units to which they can belong. What we also know is that, when

"I channeled John Dewey. He says if you want
to be a good teacher, don't teach reading
and writing. Teach students."

students cannot satisfy this need by belonging to something positive, like a family at home or an honor society in school, they will belong to something negative, like a gang. Gangs are very smart! They tell you that the gang is a *family*. Then they send you out to do something heinous, such as hurt or kill someone. That is your initiation into the *family!* The feeling one gets when belonging to a gang is no less powerful than any other organization to which one belongs. If you don't want your students in a gang, be sure that they belong to something positive, like the family of learners in your classroom.

WHY: THEORETICAL FRAMEWORK

One of the main reasons that people engage in activities that they care little about is the value placed on that activity by a person with whom they have a relationship (Jabari, 2013).

"Remember you are the alpha (leader) in the classroom. Be friendly without being a child with the children (or teenager with teens)" (Cooper & Garner, 2012, p. 43).

When teachers disclose information about their personal lives and school experiences, they cultivate emotional proximity (H. A. Davis, Gableman, & Wingfield, 2011).

"Students tend to listen more with their hearts than with their heads" (Cooper & Garner, 2012, p. 3).

Many students have to establish a relationship with their teachers before they can learn from them (Haycock, 2001; Payne, 2001).

As relationships matter when attempting to teach human beings, a person may not be able to perform as well when he or she does not feel safe with a teacher or a boss (Medina, 2008).

The brain begins to develop blueprints for adult relationships during adolescence (Feinstein, 2009).

A complicated web of social relationships that students experience with their family members, peers, and teachers have a greater effect on student behavior than was once expected (Harris, 2006).

Several studies indicate that teachers make decisions about which students to form relationships with based on student assets and obstacles. Those assets include attractiveness, social skills, and whether the student desires a relationship with the teacher (Muller, Katz, & Dance, 1999).

Because conflict is a natural consequence of learning while interacting with others, classrooms should be places where teachers model for students how to repair those relationships when they become damaged (H. A. Davis, Summers, & Miller, 2012).

HOW: CLASSROOM APPLICATION

• Relationships can begin at the door. It is at the door of the classroom where you can ask students how their weekend was, ask whether they won their game, or compliment them on a new hair style. I am at the door each time I teach my classes for adults. It is amazing how many times my participants have commented that they have been teaching for between 10 and 25 years, and this is the first time the presenter has ever been at the door. What a difference they say it makes to them! I have already begun to develop my relationship before the class even starts.

• Harry Wong and I were presenting at a conference in Canada. In a keynote speech, I heard Wong say that not only should the teacher be at the door, but one student should be standing there with the teacher to greet the class. One student greets the class for one week and then another student for the next week until every student has had an opportunity to greet the class. He related that, in schools that are doing this, bullying is decreasing significantly. It is very difficult to bully someone who has greeted you for an entire week!

• Call your students by name. A person's name is very important to his or her personal identity. I realize that this becomes much more difficult at the middle and high school level because teachers are learning the names of multiple classes of students; however, it is certainly worth a try. If you are at the door to greet daily, ask each student his or her name and then repeat it back until you learn it.

• On the first day of school, as a part of your rituals, tell the class how excited you are to have them in your community of learners for the year. For example, when addressing the class on the first day, one teacher looked at a piece of white paper, looked out at her students, looked back at the paper and at her students. She then remarked, *"This is going to be a great year! They gave me every single student I asked for!"* There was absolutely nothing on the white piece of paper. Wouldn't it be wonderful to know that your teacher actually asked for you! What a feeling of belonging!

• Allow your students to know something about you personally. This could include in which cities you have lived, schools you have attended, whether you have a spouse or children, your likes and dislikes, and so on. When I teach my math class, I turn facts about my personal life into a math word problem that teachers are only too happy to solve. By the way, developing a relationship with a student does not mean becoming his or her buddy or friend. You are the professional in the classroom and should always remain such.

• Set the ground rules for the operation of the class from day one of school. Relate that they will never hear you demean or put a student down in class and you have the same expectation for them toward one another.

- Get to know something specific about each individual student. This includes students' likes, dislikes, strengths, challenges, and interests as well as where they live, who their parents or guardians are, and what they do for a living. Knowing something about the home life of students can shed a great deal of light on the behaviors of students seen in class. Begin with those students whom you think may give you some challenges in terms of management and expand to all others. Remember that the students to whom you are least likely to give personal attention are often the ones who need that attention the most.

- Let students know that you are available to them before or after school should they need to talk with you. As students get to know and trust you, they may avail themselves of this opportunity, and you never know when a moment spent with you could possibly change a life. For example, a science teacher related to me that he noticed a change in a student's demeanor and asked her to see him after class. She related to him her detailed plans for attempting suicide. He was able to intervene and get help for her. Without a relationship, the student would never have revealed her plans to that teacher.

- Open and close class with a positive statement so that the first and last things that students hear from you leave their brains in a positive state. One high school English teacher related to me that she ends each class with the following two statements: *Have a great evening. I love you!* She said that, on the days she becomes busy and forgets to say those two sentences, her students will stand there until she remembers, or they will remind her by saying, *"You forgot to tell us you loved us!"* Remember, I said high school, not kindergarten! According to mental health professionals, a person needs 12 positive interactions per day to thrive. At least these teenagers get one of the 12 in Mrs. William's English class.

- When possible, write a positive note on the paper of a student. The note may indicate that you have noticed an improved grade over the last test, or it may relate to something personal about the student. The note is another of the 12 positive interactions that your students need to thrive.

REFLECTION

How will I build a positive
relationship with my students during
the course of the school year?

_____

_____

_____

_____

_____

_____

_____

_____

_____

_____

_____

_____

_____

_____

_____

_____

_____

_____

_____

2

Expect the Best!

*I don't become what **I** think I can!*

*I don't become what **you** think I can!*

*I become what **I** think **you** think I can!*

Kerman, S., 1979

WHAT: YOU GET WHAT YOU EXPECT

You may have noticed that, in almost every school where students change classes, there is a group of students who will be perfectly behaved in one classroom and out of control in another. Why does this happen? It may have to do with teacher expectations. You get what you expect! Students tend to live up or down to the expectations afforded them. Effective classroom managers possess the highest of expectations for student success and put plans in place to ensure that those expectations are met.

The research on expectations started in the 1960s. It began at Harvard University in the experimental psychology classroom of Dr. Robert Rosenthal. Dr. Rosenthal's students were charged with the task of getting white mice to run a maze in the shortest time possible. He divided his class into an experimental and a control group. Students in the control group were told that their mice were regular, run-of-the-mill lab mice. Students in the experimental group were told that they had carefully bred, top-of-the-line mice and to expect great things of them.

The rest is a matter of record. The mice in the experimental group ran the maze three to four times faster than those in the control group. In fact, there was no difference between the mice in the two groups. They were just randomly assigned to the experimenters; however, the students in the experimental group used more motivating and supportive interactions, and look what resulted! You get what you expect!

Robert Rosenthal teamed with a researcher by the name of Lenore Jacobson to ascertain whether what worked in the laboratory would work in a school system. They told specific groups of teachers in the Los Angeles County schools that they were being given students who had been identified by a test as late bloomers and to expect great achievement from these students this particular year. Other groups of teachers were told nothing out of the ordinary. Well, you guessed it! The students whose teachers expected great things far exceeded those whose teachers did not have the same high expectations—not only on achievement tests but measures of aptitude as well. The study became the noteworthy *Pygmalion in the Classroom* (Rosenthal & Jacobson, 1992). You get what you expect!

I realized several years ago that my sisters and I are products of high expectations. My parents and grandparents expected great things from us academically. They set the bar high, and we exceeded it. Our father used to tell us that, in school, the grade of C on a report card meant fair and that he was not raising fair children but exceptional ones. When three girls hear those words long enough over a stretch of years, they come to believe it. My older sister and I have earned doctorates, and my younger sister is the human resources manager for the Atlanta Symphony Orchestra and its subsidiaries. Our teachers also expected great things from us, and as a result, classmates of ours became teachers, ministers, doctors, lawyers, and so on. You get what you expect!

Teachers who are exceptional classroom managers expect that their students will be well disciplined and put a proactive plan in place to ensure that their expectations are met. You will never hear them make the following statements: *What else can you expect from these kids? Johnny is disrespectful, but he has no parental support and is doing the best he can! I have the worst seventh-grade class in the school!* And guess what? These teachers get what they expect!

A time-tested program called Teacher Expectations and Student Achievement (TESA) delineates 15 interactions that teachers can practice to communicate the highest of expectations to their students. These interactions include who the teacher calls on to respond to questions or to participate in

"My teacher says I'm an underachiever, but I think she"s an overexpecter."

class, how much waiting time is allowed from the time a question is asked until an answer is expected, whether the teacher delves or assists students in coming up with the correct answer, where the teacher stands in the room, how courteous the teacher is, and how much personal interest the teacher takes in each student. More than 50 years of research shows that, when these 15 interactions are practiced with every student, amazing results follow. Academic achievement is increased for all students, absenteeism is reduced, and behavior concerns diminish. For more information on this Phi Delta Kappa–sanctioned program, consult the Los Angeles County Office of Education at 800–566–6651.

WHY: THEORETICAL FRAMEWORK

A teacher's expectations are the greatest predictors of actual outcomes in the classroom (Allen & Currie, 2012).

Teachers should not lower their expectations to make it appear that students are successful when they are not. Instead, they should help students see that the route to achieving the expectation is attainable (Cooper & Garner, 2012).

Teachers with high expectations could be thought of as difficult or very demanding, but they feel the end result is worth it (Orange, 2005).

The self-filling prophecy is communicated to students through two forms of communication—explicit messages (i.e., what teachers try to say consciously) and implicit messages (i.e., what teachers say unconsciously) (H. A. Davis et al., 2012).

Labeling students with positive qualities while telling them how you expect them to act builds self-esteem and strengthens the relationship between teacher and student (Koenig, 2000).

Students will customarily rise to the expectations of their teacher (Burden, 2000).

People in the power structure of a society look for other people who resemble themselves, resulting in a closed system. Closed systems create a self-fulfilling prophecy (Sternberg & Grigorenko, 2000).

When teachers expect positive results from their classes, they will expend energy making those results happen. When teachers expect negative results, they expend just as much energy on failure (Wong & Wong, 1998).

HOW: CLASSROOM APPLICATION

- Find ways to communicate to your class that you have the highest of expectations for them. Tell them from day one of school that they are one of the smartest and most well-behaved groups of students you have had the pleasure of working with and that you will not settle for anything less. Refer to them as *bright, gifted, wonderful,* and *a joy to teach,* and mean it! Watch them live up to your expectations!

• Create the expectation that courteous behavior is the norm in your classroom, regardless of whether students practice courtesy at home. Model courtesy at every possible moment. Use words like *good morning, please, thank you, I'm sorry,* and *excuse me* with all students. Insist that students use the same courteous words with you and one another. Do not allow words of discourtesy such as *shut up, you idiot, talk to the hand, that's stupid,* and so on when students are a part of your class.

• One of the major reasons that students are hesitant to respond in class is their fear of being embarrassed. From day one of school, establish the expectation that no student in class will be put down because of an incorrect answer. Tell students that our purpose in being in school is to learn and, in some cases, to learn from our mistakes. Tell them that some of the greatest inventions started out as mistakes. Examples would be the formula for Coca Cola or the sticky notes that are used throughout the world. Set an example by never using sarcastic language or demeaning gestures with students. Remember, only 7% of your message comes from the words you say; the other 93% comes from your nonverbals (body language and gestures). In addition, don't allow students to ridicule or demean one another when an error is made. Establish your classroom as a community of learners.

• Watch where you stand in the classroom. Effective teachers with high expectations *teach on their feet and not in their seats.* If you don't assign seats, you will find that students who feel good about their abilities will often choose to sit along the front row or in the middle of the room. Students who don't feel as capable will sit at the back of the room. Place yourself in close proximity to all students by walking the room. Stand near every student in the class at some point during the lesson.

• Being near students during independent seatwork enables you to communicate your high expectations and provide students with individual assistance when necessary. A technique by Fred Jones (2000) called *praise, prompt, and leave* allows you to help more students in a shorter period of time. The three steps in this techniques are as follows: (1) When you look at a student's independent seatwork, make a positive comment or *praise* statement about what has been done so far; (2) if there is an error, provide a clue or *prompt* to move the student in the direction of a better answer; (3) then *leave* that student and move on to the next student. If the prompt in step two is not sufficient, assign a close partner or another student to work with the student needing the help. This frees you to quickly determine whether students actually understand or if reteaching is necessary.

• When a student misbehaves, label that student with a positive attribute and then state specifically what you expect of him or her; for example,

"Kathy, you are a thoughtful person. I expect you to tell Sandra that you are sorry" (Koenig, 2000).

• Ask questions at all levels of Bloom's Taxonomy so that the expectation is communicated that all students are capable of answering both *easy* and *difficult* questions. As you teach and test, make certain to include questions from the knowledge, comprehension, application, analysis, synthesis, and evaluation levels. For example, let's take the story of *Goldilocks and the Three Bears.* A knowledge question would be "Which bear's chair got broken?" While there is nothing wrong with that question, it is the lowest level of the taxonomy. Higher-level tasks would include the following: Place the events in the order in which they happened in the story (comprehension); predict what would have happened if Goldilocks had been caught by the bears (application); identify the theme of this fairy tale (analysis); create a different ending to this story (synthesis); defend Goldilocks's right to be in the home of the three bears (evaluation).

• I have taught classes in which I randomly called on a student and the student looked at me and asked, "Why did you call on me? I didn't have my hand raised." Communicate your high expectations to all students by creating the expectation that both volunteers and non-volunteers will be called upon to participate. Use random ways of involving students, such as writing their names on Popsicle sticks or index cards, placing those sticks or cards in a can or box, and pulling a student's stick or card whenever a question is asked or involvement needed. Some teachers use a computer program that randomly flashes students' names on a screen.

• One teacher I observed made a bingo board out of her classroom by having students sit in five straight rows with five students in each row. Instead of using the word *bingo,* she used the word *learn.* Therefore, if a student was sitting in row 1, seat 3, that student was in seat L3. At the front of the room was a canister containing the chips of all the seats in the room. Whenever student involvement was needed, the teacher reached in, pulled out a chip, and the chip designated the student who would respond. How motivating this method of participation was for this seventh-grade class!

• One of the reasons for students' incorrect answers is an inadequate amount of time between the time a teacher asks a question and the time the teacher expects the answer. Research shows that, if teachers have high expectations, they will wait approximately 2.6 seconds, but if teachers have low expectations, they will wait less than 1 second (Kerman, 1979). Provide a minimum of 5 seconds of quiet from the time you ask a question until the time you expect an answer. Allowing more time for thinking results in more comprehensive answers and an expectation that all students are capable of giving quality responses.

• When a student answers a question incorrectly, or not at all, provide wait time as outlined above. If the student's answer is still inappropriate, rephrase the question, provide additional information, or give clues to move the student in the direction of the right answer.

REFLECTION

> **What is my plan for communicating my highest expectations to all of my students?**

_____

_____

_____

_____

_____

_____

_____

_____

_____

_____

_____

_____

_____

_____

_____

_____

_____

_____

_____

3

Understand the Symptoms

Even the worst-behaving child is acting that way because he or she is receiving something useful from the misbehavior.

Kottler, 2002

WHAT: CAUSES OF MISBEHAVIOR

Patrick is constantly calling your name. Even when he knows the answers to questions, he needs your assurance that his answers are correct. You are sick and tired of reprimanding him for talking out loud without being called upon first.

Melissa is demanding and argumentative. If you say the sky is blue, she says it's brown. She is always calling her peers inappropriate names and, when reprimanded, shrugs you off and refuses to listen to your requests.

Duane is bored with school and with you. He is frequently caught sleeping in class or at the very least with his head on his desk. He is unmotivated and puts out little effort. When not sleeping, he is looking for ways to bother the other students so that they cannot complete their assignments either.

When you give Gail an assignment, all you hear is *"I don't understand"* or *"I can't do this!"* She makes little effort and has literally given up. She is having great difficulty reading the grade-level texts yet does not qualify for any special programs.

When students refuse to complete assigned tasks, disrupt your class, or are disrespectful to you and others, you may be tempted to treat the symptoms with the harshest of penalties. While there certainly should be consequences for misbehavior, effective classroom managers look beyond the symptoms to find the causes of the disruptions. This is why relationships are so important. It is during those relationships that you may discover some of the causes for the misbehavior.

For example, my daughter Jennifer taught a third grader who never turned in any homework. Rather than simply doling out consequences, Jenny developed a relationship with this student and learned that she was caring for three younger siblings, while her mother worked a second job in the evenings. If her brothers and sisters were not fed, bathed, and in the bed by the time her mother got home, this third grader received a spanking. What is more important—avoiding an F as a homework grade or avoiding physical punishment and the disapproval of the most important person in your life? I think you know the answer to that question.

There appear to be four major reasons for student misbehavior: desire for attention, desire for power or control, boredom, and feelings of inadequacy. Let's examine each cause independently.

1. Some students need your attention and the attention of their classmates as well. For whatever reason, they get the idea that they are either being ignored or not receiving the percentage of your time that they feel they deserve. Therefore, they will call your name a hundred times a day, tap their pencil repeatedly, or disrupt other students who may be trying to do as you have requested. When they have gotten on your last nerve, you may be tempted to engage them in a power struggle or order them out of your classroom. Did you know that negative attention is considered better than no attention at all? Therefore, even if you argue with them or banish them to another location in the building, they have received the attention they seek. After all, every student in your class is giving them undivided attention as they walk out of your classroom.

2. A second reason that students misbehave involves their need for power or control. Many of your students have an inordinate amount of control in their homes. They may be raising younger brothers and sisters as well as themselves and, as a result, are *calling the shots* and making major life decisions. Then they come to school and cannot understand why everyone, including you, will not dance to their music. The opposite also exists. Some students feel that they have little or absolutely no control over their personal lives; therefore, these students exhibit characteristics of belligerence, disrespect, and downright disobedience.

3. Other students misbehave because they are just plain bored. In many classrooms, students sit for long periods of time without any active engagement of their brains or bodies. Their brains are not getting enough oxygen, and they may either yawn repeatedly, fall asleep, or think of other things while the lesson is being taught. They may also randomly hit a classmate simply because they cannot think of anything better to do or because they would like to inject a little excitement into their day.

4. The fourth reason students disrupt has to do with their feelings of inadequacy. They really cannot do what you are requesting of them. Their brains do not have the confidence to believe that they are capable of being successful on the assigned task; therefore, they do things to divert attention away from their poor performance. After all, it is better to be considered the class clown than the class dummy! No one wants to be considered inadequate.

You can deal with difficult students if you first recognize their primary needs (Canter & Canter, 1993). Once you look beyond the symptoms of misbehavior, you may discover the causes. Simply treating the symptoms may stop them temporarily. However, if there is to be meaningful behavior change, a deeper inspection is warranted.

WHY: THEORETICAL FRAMEWORK

When a student's need for social recognition is not satisfied, he or she can display the following goals of misbehavior: attention, power or control, revenge, and inadequacy (Pinto, 2013).

For some students in middle school, any attention (positive or negative) is better than remaining anonymous because it is proof that they exist and affirms their sense of being (Allen & Currie, 2012).

Students who need attention are often either kinesthetic or visual learners who do not learn best when the instruction is predominately auditory (Tileston, 2004).

When students seek attention, teachers feel annoyed. However, when students seek power and control, teachers feel threatened (Tileston, 2004).

When students act out, it is a call for help. When teachers understand and address these calls, they provide students with the best opportunities to make meaningful changes in behavior (Smith, 2004).

Students whose feelings of power come from a sense of autonomy are more likely to stick with an instructional task and experience long-term benefits from it (Ryan & Deci, 2000).

Boredom breeds bad behavior (Allen & Currie, 2012).

If students are behaving badly because they are bored, the one way to solve the problem is to incorporate strategies that actively engage their brains (Jensen, 2009).

When 81,000 high school students were asked about their daily school experiences, approximately one-half of all students reported being bored every single day (Yazzie-Mintz, 2007).

Students should never be allowed to feel that their misbehavior is ignored or condoned simply because they have difficulties in their lives (Cooper & Garner, 2012).

HOW: CLASSROOM APPLICATION

- Get to know each of your students personally in an effort to understand why they behave as they do. Begin with those students who may appear to give you more of a challenge than others. Once you comprehend what some of your students are experiencing, you may become more sympathetic to their challenging behavior and comprehend why they act as they do.

- Students who seek attention need attention. However, give them the attention when they are doing what is expected of them. Provide them with special recognition when you see them meeting expectations. Compliment them in front of their peers, write positive comments on their papers when their written work shows improvement, and provide them with privileges that indicate growth. In the case of middle or high school students, special recognitions may be given in a private, rather than public, setting.

- Providing students with choice can give them some measure of control. Allow them to choose among several options for completing an assignment or responding to an assessment task.

- Students who seek control need to be given it. Put these students, along with others, into positions of responsibility. Make them line leaders, cooperative group facilitators, and peer teachers. With your supervision, allow them to teach a lesson to the class. You may very well have to equip them with the social skills necessary to get along with peers because many students who seek control exhibit few interpersonal skills. See Chapter 14 for specific directions on teaching your social skills to students.

- By using the 20 brain-compatible strategies outlined in the bestseller *Worksheets Don't Grow Dendrites: 20 Instructional Strategies That Engage the Brain,* 2nd edition (Tate, 2010), students in your classroom will become actively engaged in learning. When they have opportunities to role-play vocabulary words, move to meet with a discussion partner, complete a project, or play a content-related game, students do not have time to be bored, and their behavior naturally improves. These strategies appear to work for all student populations including gifted, regular education, special education, and ESL.

- Students who believe themselves to be inadequate need confidence. Often, these students develop major behavior problems because they cloak their inadequacies with inappropriate behavior. Give these students successful experiences by providing work at an appropriate instructional level. As they begin to experience success, they will want to take on more challenging assignments. The 20 strategies mentioned previously are the best way to increase understanding and retention of information for all students, including those performing significantly below grade level.

- As a reading specialist, I often worked with students who were considerably below grade level in reading performance. They felt totally inadequate to deal with grade-level text. I had to begin by teaching them at their instructional levels in an effort to instill confidence in their ability to read. As the students experienced success, their brains gained confidence. It was amazing how quickly we progressed through more challenging material.

- I cannot figure out how some teachers get the mistaken idea that, if a student has a history of failing grades, he or she will be somehow motivated by receiving one more grade of F in the current class. There is nothing brain compatible or logical about that concept at all.

- Refer to Chapter 19 for additional recommendations appropriate to those students who are bored, are in need of attention, seek power or control, or feel inadequate.

REFLECTION

> What is my plan for meeting the needs
> of each of the four major types of misbehavior
> in any classroom?

Goal: Attention

_____

_____

_____

_____

Goal: Power or Control

_____

_____

_____

_____

Goal: Boredom

_____

_____

_____

_____

Goal: Inadequacy

_____

_____

_____

_____

DETOUR →

Create a Physical Environment Conducive to Learning

4

Light Up
Their World

Let there be light,
and there was light.

Genesis 1:3

WHAT: LIGHTING AND THE BRAIN

A school system was in the process of building five new schools to house their increasing student population. Having read the research on the detrimental effects of fluorescent lighting, I shared with the architects rationales for including additional windows or a different type of lighting in the construction of these new buildings. The experts thanked me for my input but proceeded to include fluorescent lighting in plans for each of the five new edifices. You see, this type of lighting is less expensive. While fiscal responsibility is certainly warranted, the increased expense may be offset by decreases in misbehavior and ill health and increases in academic achievement.

The information I shared with the architects included the facts that fluorescent lighting pulses or flickers, which some students and adults can sense. This type of light tends to make hyperactive children more hyperactive, increases the onset of migraine headaches, and can cause those who are prone to epileptic seizures to experience an increase in the frequency and severity of those seizures.

More than 60 years ago, an extensive study of 160,000 students showed that, when lighting in classrooms improved, so did student difficulties with vision, nutrition, infections, posture, and fatigue (Harmon, 1951). Additional neuroscientific research (Heschong, 1999; Jensen, 1995; MacLaughlin, Anderson, & Holic, 1982) reinforces the fact that the best light for the brain is natural light. It stands to reason that, if the purpose of the brain is to help the body survive in the world, then natural light, such as sunlight, would be optimal. If your classroom has windows, open the shades, and let the light shine through.

There are classrooms where windows are simply not an option. In fact, more and more schools are being built without windows. If this is the case in your environment, try bringing alternative lighting or lamps into your classroom. Even turning off half the fluorescent lights and supplementing with lamps is helpful. This practice alone appears to reduce behavior problems because the lower lighting calms the brain—a preferable state for optimal learning. In fact, lamps also give the classroom a homelike atmosphere, which is more natural for brains.

There are cultures in the world that experience 6 months of light and 6 months of darkness. During the dark months, alcoholism, depression, and suicide increase. Fifteen percent of the population is impacted by seasonal affective disorder (SAD), which is a form of depression that results when people are deprived of daylight for long periods of time. The symptoms usually disappear during the spring and summer months. Cognitive problems that may accompany SAD include lapses in verbal and visual memory and lack of attention (Michalon, Eskes, & Mate-Kole, 1997).

Those in the business world realize the impact of appropriate lighting. The next time you eat at a restaurant where the meal is costing you *an arm and a leg*, notice that the lights are so low that you can hardly read the menu. You are probably reading by candlelight. The owners know that you will relax and enjoy your meal a lot better if you experience a low light source. At home, when you want to relax and block out the stresses of the day, try the low lighting of a candle. Candles create a brain-compatible atmosphere conducive to calming and can make for a romantic evening. The light from a fireplace works well also. Why do you think I've been married for more than 35 years?

WHY: THEORETICAL FRAMEWORK

A less harshly lit environment can be created by using lamps or by placing colored crepe paper over fluorescent lights (Cooper & Garner, 2012).

Strong natural lighting can have a dramatic and lasting effect on the learning environment (Jensen, 2008).

In a 2007 study of 21,000 students, those classrooms with the greatest amount of sunlight had students whose progress exceeded that of their peers by 20% in math and 26% in reading (Heschong Mahone Group, 2012).

Fluorescent lights possess a flicker and barely discernible hum, which raises the cortisol, or stress, levels in the central nervous system of students (Jensen, 2008).

Inadequate or inappropriate lighting, air, and heat can influence behavior (Tileston, 2004).

Bright fluorescent lights appeared to create restless, overactive learners while lower-level lighting appeared to calm students (Jensen, 1995).

Students in brightly lit classrooms perform better than students in dimly lit classrooms (London, 1988).

HOW: CLASSROOM APPLICATION

• If you have windows in your classroom, open the shades, and let in the sunshine. It will provide your students' brains with the best source of lighting.

• If your classroom has fluorescent lighting with two separate light switches, turn off half the fluorescent lights, and supplement with lamps. This procedure will reduce the impact of a detrimental light source and provide a lower, softer source of illumination.

• If it is not a violation of a fire code, try placing pastel-colored crepe paper over the fluorescent lights in the ceiling. The paper will put a color barrier between the harsh flicker of the ceiling lights and the brains of your students.

• If you only have one switch to your fluorescent lights, turn it off, and bring lamps into your classroom. Certain types of floor lamps may have several separate light sources and can be directed to different areas of the room, thereby providing illumination to more students. If lamps do not provide sufficient lighting, explore the possibility of unscrewing the bulbs in half of your fluorescent lights and using a combination of both ceiling lights and lamps.

• Several teachers whom I have observed allow their students to wear baseball caps in class to deflect the negative effects of fluorescent lighting. The bill of the cap causes the light to be deflected and not shine directly into the student's line of vision. Students are only allowed to wear the caps in class but must remove them before going into the hall or cafeteria.

• Convene some classes outdoors so that students can take advantage of the natural ultraviolet light from the sun. The research is showing that doctors may have to start prescribing doses of Vitamin D for today's children because they are not getting sufficient doses of it from playing outdoors in the sun.

• When students are not getting a sufficient amount of light, and you are unable to take them outside, allow them to engage in movement connected to learning and other types of physical activity in the room. The activity will produce positive chemicals in the brain, such as epinephrine and dopamine, which can combat depression.

• Get your brain in a state of calm by relaxing with candles or the light from a fireplace at home. Candlelight in combination with appropriate music and aromas will reduce stress and create an atmosphere conducive to relaxation. After all, a stress-free, good night's sleep helps to prepare both brain and body to be a successful classroom manager on the following day.

REFLECTION

> What is my plan for providing
> appropriate *lighting* in my classroom?

_____

_____

_____

_____

_____

_____

_____

_____

_____

_____

_____

_____

_____

_____

_____

_____

_____

_____

5

Let the Music Play

Music has charms to soothe a savage breast,
to soften rocks, or bend a knotted oak.

Congreve

WHAT: MUSIC AND THE BRAIN

I simply cannot teach or live without music! Neither should you. Music gets each day off to an encouraging start, leads students calmly through transition times, minimizes classroom disruptions, and gives all who hear it a sense of well-being. Bringing the right kind of music into your classroom can alleviate at least 50 percent of your classroom management concerns because it can make the hyperactive student less hyper and the angry student less angry.

In perusing the research on the power of music to affect the brain, you will find three major concepts. First, there tends to be a correlation between a person's ability to solve problems, particularly in mathematics, and his or her ability to play a musical instrument (College Board, 2012; Covino, 2002). My daughter Jessica is an example of this fact. Jessica took piano lessons for 10 years, played the trombone in the band, learned to sight read music, and sang in both the chorus and chamber chorus in high school and college. She also obtained a very high score on the mathematics portion of the Scholastic Aptitude Test (SAT) and speaks German fluently. I do believe that all the years of music training strengthened the spatial part of her brain, which enabled her to excel at higher levels of math and fluently speak a second language.

The second advantage of music lies in the fact that music helps you remember (Feinstein, 2009; Jensen, 2001; Sprenger, 2010). If you don't believe that music facilitates memory, you will not be able to complete this phrase. I bet you can do it! Fill in the blank: *Conjunction junction*, _____. If you answered, *What's your function?*, then you are like the millions of people who were taught by the cartoon characters and catchy tunes of *Schoolhouse Rock*. I learned more English and history watching that show on Saturday mornings than I learned in my elementary and high school classes. Music is still being used today to teach students to remember content and is one of the 20 strategies that I have identified as correlating with the way brains learn best.

However, the best use of music for classroom management is for calming students down and getting their brains in a state for learning (Erlauer, 2003; Sousa, 2006). The old saying "music has charms to soothe a savage breast" is not only true, but it is pervasive. I have experienced many classrooms, at all grade levels, in which students enter each morning or every period to some type of calming music playing softly in the background. Calming music includes some forms of classical, jazz, new age, Celtic, or spiritual, such as Native American flute music. Students can be taught that, if their voices can be heard over the music, then they are talking too loudly.

Many school personnel have forbidden students to talk in the cafeteria. Names are taken, and students pay harsh penalties all in the name of silent lunch. While you might disagree with this statement, I will make it anyway. I have come to the conclusion that it is unnatural to eat lunch with someone and not desire to talk with him or her. When is the last time that you went out to lunch or dinner with a friend and were not allowed to talk to him or her? Are we expecting behaviors of students that would not be characteristic of or appropriate for adults?

"I downloaded music from a radio station in
South Korea, and I got Seoul music."

SOURCE: Copyright 2007, Aaron Bacall, *The Lighter Side of Classroom Management*, Thousand Oaks, CA: Corwin. May not be reproduced without permission in writing from the artist, Aaron Bacall.

A better plan would be to have some type of calming music playing softly in the cafeteria throughout the lunch period and to have teachers instruct their students in the proper voice tone and etiquette one should use when dining with friends. In this way, they would be equipping their students with lifelong skills for successful dining.

Music can also change the state of the brain to one of enthusiasm and motivation. Visualize how engaged one gets when hearing the popular song "Happy" from the movie *Despicable Me 2* or the song "We Will Rock You!" I received an e-mail from an art teacher who related the following incident. He had attended one of my workshops and was having a difficult time getting his art students to clean up following the completion of their art projects. He found himself shouting at students to get the classroom cleaned up prior to the ringing of the bell each period. After hearing about the motivational aspects of music, the teacher decided to have students clean to the melodic rhythm of the song "Car Wash" by Rose Royce. What a difference! Students were now competing to be the first to finish cleaning before the song ended each period.

A police officer in a major U.S. city attended one of my workshops with his wife, a building principal. He related the true story of barbers in the city who appealed to the police department to get rid of the drug dealers who were hanging out on the corner outside of their shop, or they would have to close due to lack of business. The police officer, who had read about the beneficial aspects of classical music, began playing it in the shop loud enough for the drug dealers to hear on the outside. He related that, in two days, the drug dealers were gone! He told me that he has aspirations of writing a book. Instead of being called *Stop or I'll Shoot*, the book would be called *Stop or I'll Play Vivaldi!* I think he is onto something!

WHY: THEORETICAL FRAMEWORK

When a teacher is doing direct instruction, music (calming or otherwise) should be turned off so that the teacher doesn't have to compete with the music (Allen & Wood, 2013).

Turning music on and off can be a signal to students that they should be ready for what is happening next in class (Sprenger, 2010).

Using music as a volume barrier while students are collaborating keeps the noise levels during cooperative learning activities to a minimum (Allen & Currie, 2012).

Popular and classical music can be used to create a variety of moods in the classroom, while students can create rhythms, lyrics, and raps to remember information (Cooper & Garner, 2012).

Rhythmic processes of the human body, such as breathing and heart rate, synchronize with the beat of music (Allen & Wood, 2013).

(Continued)

(Continued)

Fast-paced music motivates students and causes them to move, while calming, soothing music can settle them down (Allen & Currie, 2012).

Music composed during the Baroque period averages 45 to 60 beats per minute and can balance both the body and mind, thereby regulating respiration, heart rate, and brain waves, resulting in a state of relaxation for the listener (Sprenger, 2010).

Music can reduce stress, stimulate thinking, reduce behavior problems, and align the energy of the group (Jensen, 2008).

Because various types of music create different psychophysiological states in students, a variety of music should be used (Jensen, 2008).

While the type of music played for the teenage brain does not appear to make an academic or emotional difference, combining that music with pictures in a video may have a more powerful or even detrimental effect (Feinstein, 2009).

"The beat of the music can provide the ADHD student with a *landing strip* on which they can connect their ideas and organize information coming into the brain" (Willis, 2007, p. 70).

Teenage musicians are less likely to engage in at-risk activities such as drug use (Costa-Giomi, 1998).

Patients recovering from alcohol or chemical addictions related that chronic stress was decreased following treatment sessions when music and visualization were combined (Hammer, 1996).

HOW: CLASSROOM APPLICATION

• Begin a collection of music of a variety of genres (Baroque, jazz, Celtic, salsa, big band, country, positive rap, etc.). CDs with collections of music from the 1960s, 1970s, and 1980s are particularly effective because the tunes are catchy and the majority of the lyrics are not objectionable.

• Don't be surprised if students object to the introduction of types of music to which they are not accustomed, such as classical or jazz. Teachers relate, however, that if they persist in their use of music, any day that they forget to turn it on, students will ask for it.

• If you do not wish to be charged with the responsibility of turning on the music daily, assign this task to a student whose sole job is to be your disc jockey for the week. Students could take turns with this task and may even wish to bring in appropriate music for the class to hear.

• As your students enter your room each day or each period, have some type of calming music playing to get their brains in a state for learning. Teach them that, as they assemble, their voices should not be heard over the music. Role-play the appropriate way to talk while listening to music, and have your class practice this skill until they get it right. Classical, smooth jazz, Celtic, Native American music, and nature sounds all tend to be calming for most brains.

- Use energizing music when you want to invigorate, energize, or actively engage your class. Music with an upbeat tempo will wake up those brain cells and get the oxygen and blood pumping. This type of music can be playing while students are walking around the room in search of a partner with whom to discuss content or completing a high-energy activity such as drawing or using manipulatives. Country, salsa, rock and roll, rhythm and blues, and positive rap all fit the bill for a more energizing type of music.

- Select songs that fit the content of the unit of study. Music can peak interest and minimize behavior concerns. For example, when studying a period of history, play samples of accompanying music from that period. Play the theme from *Welcome Back, Kotter* to greet students following a long weekend or a holiday.

- Use music to assist you in setting time limits on assigned activities. For example, students must complete an activity by the time a specific song ends. Watch how motivated students become when trying to beat the music!

- Allow students to work individually or with peers to create a song, rhyme, rap, or poem that demonstrates their understanding of content. This is an engaging way to have students mentally rehearse what has been taught and uses one of the highest-level thinking skills—synthesis.

- Celebrate academic and behavioral successes in your classroom with appropriate music. Songs like "We Are the Champions" by Queen, "Celebration" by Kool and the Gang, and "I Got the Power" by Snap all get students' brains fired up and excited when good things happen as students acquire new concepts and score well on measures of assessment.

- Consult the extensive list of music for all occasions in the books *Top Tunes for Teaching* by Eric Jensen (2005b) and *The Rock 'N' Roll Classroom* by Rich Allen and W. W. Wood (2013).

- Remember that the majority of class time (approximately 60 to 70 percent) is spent without music. If music is played as students are writing or concentrating, keep the volume low so as not to disturb their thought processes. Be aware of students who have difficulty concentrating when there is any music played at all. In this case, music may be played only during transition times or headphones may be used by students who need them.

REFLECTION

> ## What are the most appropriate times
> ## for incorporating *music* into my classroom?

_____

_____

_____

_____

_____

Calming Music

_____

_____

_____

_____

_____

High-Energy Music

_____

_____

_____

_____

_____

_____

6

Color
Their World

In general, we remember color first and content second.

Jensen, 2008, p. 56

WHAT: COLOR AND THE BRAIN

Have you ever stopped to think about how the colors in this world affect you? I didn't think much about it until I made a mistake with color in my home. My husband and I dined with friends who had just moved into a beautiful new house. Their dining room was painted a cranberry color that provided an elegance to the already exquisite surroundings. We were so enamored of the wall color that we went home and painted the walls in our den the same color. For us, this was a definite mistake! While cranberry was surely appropriate for the high-energy dining room in the home of our friends, it was not as applicable for the high ceilings in the den of our home. You see, the den had always been a calming place for the family to be. It was suddenly transformed into a high-energy room where no one chose to be anymore. Even our three children were not sitting in the den. We hastily repainted our den a hunter green, and everyone in the family returned to what had at one time been our favorite room in the house.

Not too long after this incident, I began reading brain research that explained exactly what had happened. Educators are only beginning to comprehend what people in advertising have known for a long time: that color influences emotion, behavior, mood, and even cognition (Jensen & Dabney, 2000).

I learned that reds (even cranberry), oranges, and deep yellows are high-energy colors for the brain. This is why most of the fast-food restaurants, such as Kentucky Fried Chicken, Burger King, and McDonald's, are painted these colors. I have even noticed that, on the television weather forecast, when there is a preponderance of intense weather such as rain or wind, the color on the map where the weather is most severe is red, next severe is orange, and so on.

If high-energy colors excite, which colors calm? As the brain was designed to exist in the world, wouldn't it make sense for the colors in nature to be the most calming colors for the brain? For example, the sky is blue, the grass is green, the earth is brown, and if we look at the rainbow from earth, it looks pastel. Therefore, blues, greens, earth tones, and pastels are among the most calming colors for each brain. However, nature even handles the high-energy colors. Just look at the beautiful red, orange, and deep yellow leaves changing in the fall!

Color can even be beneficial for some readers. Pastel-colored overlays placed on top of an assignment or a book that a student is reading can be beneficial for those who experience what the research calls *Irlen syndrome.* According to Rickelman and Henk (1990), this practice can provide many at-risk students with the chance that they need to be successful. In one research study, after only 1 week, those students who read with an appropriately colored transparency placed on top of their reading gained 6.6 months in reading achievement and 19.35 months in comprehension (O'Connor, Sofo, Kendall, & Olsen, 1990). These transparencies are usually light blue or yellow in color. To find additional information on *Irlen syndrome,* contact the researcher, Helen Irlen, via her website at www.irlen .com or e-mail at Irleninstitutc@Irlcn.com.

The house that we live in now is very brain compatible. Each room is a different shade of beige or brown, and no matter what room we are in, we experience a sense of satisfaction and peace. After all, I learned my lesson regarding color the hard way!

WHY: THEORETICAL FRAMEWORK

Research indicates that the earth tone colors of brown, green, and blue can facilitate memory, while reds, oranges, and yellows can be used for emphasis (Cooper & Garner, 2012).

The more colorful the imagery is when we initially experience a task, the more easily we can use similar images when we attempt to recall the learning situation at a later time (Jensen & Dabney, 2000).

Evidence suggests that boys, in particular, respond more positively to strong, visual stimuli that are enhanced with color (Bender, 2012).

Mixing colors can help students retain information that is presented in a list (Cooper & Garner, 2012).

Underlining key words and important concepts with colored markers improves semantic memory and visual recognition (Jensen & Dabney, 2000).

Preschool students who experienced wall colors that appealed to them as well as other positive environmental changes cooperated more after their exposure than before (Read, Sugawara, & Brandt, 1999).

When colors are used in close proximity to words in texts, colors can enhance a student's memory of the texts (Wallace, West, Ware, & Dansereau, 1998).

Color is being used successfully to reduce stress and create a sense of well-being in health care facilities (Frasca-Beaulieu, 1999).

Fifty years ago, it was found that the warm, shortwave colors of red, orange, and yellow tended to arouse people even if they didn't appear pleasing. The cool, long-wave colors of blues and greens tended to have a more calming effect (Shaie & Heiss, 1964).

HOW: CLASSROOM APPLICATION

• Use high-energy colors such as red, orange, or deep yellow to motivate or excite students. Many primary classrooms are replete with colorful rugs and bulletin boards that catch the eye of the students and create an air of excitement in the room.

• Use calming colors such as blues, greens, pastels, or earth tones to create a more relaxing classroom atmosphere.

• Blue dry-erase or permanent markers are preferable for writing on the board, document camera, or a flip chart. However, for emphasis, use red markers. For example, if you want your students to focus on the punctuation marks in a sentence, write the sentence in blue and the punctuation marks in red.

• When grading papers, use more calming markers such as blue or green to make comments or correct mistakes. Red tends to be more alarming and offensive to the brain, particularly when it is coupled with negative remarks or recommendations.

• Have students who need them place pastel-colored acetate sheets on top of their textbooks or stark white paper when reading. Some students have improved focus and reading performance when looking through these colored sheets. Different students will read best with different colors, so keep a set of various colors in the classroom.

• Place colored markers or pencils on the school supply list for your students. Have them use these markers or colored pencils to underline important concepts or key words and phrases in their notes for emphasis. Color will call attention to crucial notes and make them easier for the brain to recall.

- Thinking, concept, mind, and semantic maps are types of graphic organizers that appeal to both left and right hemispheres of the brain. They are pictorial representations of linear ideas. Adding color to these mind maps only increases their effectiveness and impact on students' comprehension and retention. Markowitz and Jensen (2007) describe the four steps involved in creating a mind map:

  o Get a large sheet of paper and colored markers.
  o Draw the central topic or main idea on the paper.
  o Add lines coming out of the central topic to depict key ideas or subtopics.
  o Make it personal by doodling, illustrating, or using symbols to assist the brain in recalling the information.

- Have students add color to their computer graphics, reports, presentations, and projects for increased appeal and better retention.

REFLECTION

> ### What is my plan for incorporating appropriate *color* into my classroom?

7

Stop and Smell the Roses

*A human being's sense of smell is one of
the most direct pathways to the brain.*

Dhong, Chung, & Doty, 1999

WHAT: AROMAS AND THE BRAIN

Have you noticed that when you smell a particular odor, memories come flooding back? Maybe it's a scent from your childhood that brings to mind your mother cooking one of your favorite foods in the family kitchen. Maybe it's a fragrance that a particular person wears, and when you smell it, all of the memories of your experiences with that person are recalled.

Your sense of smell is the sense most strongly related to memory. People are keenly aware of the circumstances associated with smells. Did you know, however, that certain smells can calm the brain, and others can excite or invigorate the brain, while still others have the ability to improve concentration and memory?

Before we begin this discussion, be aware that certain students in your classroom may have allergies. You will not want to do anything to cause a student to become uncomfortable or to aggravate his or her allergies. Therefore, take this fact into consideration when using aromas in your classroom. If you do have such a student, then use the information regarding aromas to make your house a more inviting place. That is exactly what I did.

When I worked in the Department of Professional Development with the DeKalb County School System, I had a metal ring placed on a lightbulb in my office. I poured lavender oil into the metal ring. Whenever I turned on that lamp, the lightbulb would heat the metal ring, sending the aroma of lavender into the air. Lavender has a very calming effect on the brain, so the combination of classical music played on my CD player, low lighting, and a rock garden in the corner made my office a calming and brain-compatible place. People would come into my office and not want to leave. However, the lavender bothered the allergies of a person in my department, so I discontinued its use.

Today, in my home, I have scented plug-ins in the bedrooms and ceramic pots in the larger room. In the bottom of the ceramic pots, I have tea lights, or the pots plug into the wall to be heated. In the tops of the pots, I have my favorite liquid scents. My favorite aromas come out only twice a year. The scent *autumn leaves* comes out at Thanksgiving, and the scent *balsam and cedar* only appears on the store shelves at Christmas, so I buy enough of both fragrances for the entire year at those times. Needless to say, after a busy week of traveling, I look forward to coming home to a relaxing environment, and aromas add to that atmosphere.

WHY: THEORETICAL FRAMEWORK

Preliminary evidence points to a positive correlation between smell and cognition (Jensen, 2008).

Because smells stimulate areas in the brain responsible for creating memories and emotions, aromas appear to have become a centerpiece in the positive correlation between human sensory response and marketing (Medina, 2008).

Undergraduate students performed better in word-association and word-naming tasks after being exposed to the odors of vanilla and lavender (Pauli, Bourne, Diekmann, & Birbaumer, 1999; Schnaubelt, 1999).

Environmental smells can affect our mood, fear, hunger, depression, and learning as there appears to be a direct link between the nervous system and the olfactory glands (Jensen, 2008).

Scientists have known for more than 100 years that smells can evoke long-lost memories. This theory is known as the *Proust effect* (Medina, 2008).

Adding a scent of lemon to the classroom helps to involve all of the senses in student experiences (Feinstein, 2004).

Our sense of smell generates feelings of pleasure and well-being because the olfactory regions in the brain are rich receptors for endorphins (Jensen, 2008).

The brain processes the sense of smell unlike any of the other physical senses; therefore, that sense enjoys undisturbed, unfiltered access to the brain (Jensen, 2007).

The emotion connected with *odor-evoked memory* stimulates the amygdala when students are trying to recall content and influences the organization of that content (Herz, Eliassen, Beland, & Souza, 2004).

A person's sense of smell is directly tied to the frontal lobe of the brain, which controls willpower and the limbic system, where memories and emotions are housed (van Toller, 1988).

HOW: CLASSROOM APPLICATION

• Poll your class to ensure that students are not allergic to specific fragrances. If any student falls into that category, you will have to use the information in this chapter in your personal, rather than professional, life.

• Use peppermint, cinnamon, and citrus (especially lemon and orange) scents to energize students late in the school day. Thyme and rosemary are also energizing fragrances.

• Use lavender, jasmine, vanilla, chamomile, or eucalyptus to calm the brains of students and reduce stress. Calming fragrances paired with calming music can relieve a large percentage of your discipline concerns.

• If you have students who are allergic to certain fragrances and you, therefore, cannot place them in the room for all to smell, purchase a *car jar*. Car jars are individual packets of specific aromas that students can smell, but the fragrance is not pervasive enough to cover the room. Place the car jar at one place in the room (away from any student who is allergic), and allow students to get up one at a time and take a sniff when needed.

• Eliminate unpleasant odors; they tend to negatively impact learning because the sense of smell is tied to the brain's frontal lobe and limbic system.

• Following a busy or stressful school day, use the same fragrances of lavender, jasmine, vanilla, chamomile, or eucalyptus plug-ins at home to relax.

• Another aromatherapy technique, which can be used at home, consists of placing a tea light in the bottom of a ceramic pot and placing a tart on the top of the pot. As the pot heats, the tart melts, putting the energizing or calming fragrance in the air. This technique works well if there is a great deal of room area to cover at home.

• Tarts, oils, and scents can be purchased online, at Bed Bath and Beyond, or at any other bath and body shop.

REFLECTION

> ## What is my plan for incorporating appropriate *aromas* into my classroom?

_____

_____

_____

_____

_____

_____

_____

_____

_____

_____

_____

_____

_____

_____

_____

_____

_____

_____

8

Create a Natural Environment

A 21st century classroom bears a striking resemblance to a home environment.

Marcia L. Tate

WHAT: ROOM ARRANGEMENT AND THE BRAIN

Your brain has but one purpose: to help your body survive in the *real* world. Notice that I wrote *in the real world.* In reality, the body is not confined to a wooden or metal desk 5 to 6 hours per day. Even if adults have desk jobs in the real world of work, no boss stands over them and demands that they stay at the desk until break or lunch time. The body is allowed to sit and stand and bend and flex and recline and lie down, but this is not so in most classrooms.

School is a very artificial place for both brain and body. Recess and nap time are even being taken away from little ones in the name of increased time on task and academic achievement. In many classrooms, older students sit in uncomfortable desks unless it is time for lunch, physical education, or a change of classes. We often wonder why boys, particularly, are out of their seats or leaning with one knee in the desk and the other foot on the floor. Perhaps boys are even more uncomfortable with continuous sitting than are girls, but they do not want to be in trouble for being out of their seats. I am even convinced that, when students ask to go to the bathroom, it is not that they need to go. They just need to move!

When I teach staff development classes, adults will often come up before class and ask my permission to stand or take breaks during instruction due to recurring back problems or other health issues. I always consent because I want my adult learners to be as comfortable as possible. What if I responded to their requests with the comment, *"You must stay in your seat during instruction. I am sorry about your health issues."* Do you think their brains would be in much of a state to hear what I had to say following that response? I think not!

As long as students do not infringe on the rights of their peers, they should be offered flexible seating options. What would be wrong with offering students multiple opportunities to move while learning? In fact, moving places the information in one of the strongest memory systems in the brain—procedural memory (Jensen, 2003; Sprenger, 2002). See Chapter 12 for additional research on the benefits of movement for the brain.

When students must be seated, why not provide some alternatives to desks such as tables and chairs, carpet squares on the floor, an old sofa, or a beanbag chair. What would be wrong with letting students stand for short periods? As a fourth-grade teacher, I had a podium in the back of my classroom so that, if students needed to stand and write, they could take the opportunity to do so. Some teachers provide rocking chairs for those attention-deficit disordered students whose brains might appreciate a little extra movement. In some classrooms, students actually bounce around on large balls to provide more consistent movement for their brains and bodies.

Contrary to popular belief, providing some seating alternatives for students will not increase your classroom management concerns. If the movement is purposeful, structured, and organized within the context of the lesson, this technique will actually reduce the number of behavior challenges. Students will learn with more comfort, and their brains will simultaneously produce dopamine—the neurotransmitter that assists them in focusing and paying attention.

Different desk arrangements can provide novelty to the brain as well. Students can be shown how to move their seats into different configurations, depending on what the subsequent activity requires. Once shown,

"I want you to sit up front right by my
desk. It's not because I want to keep an eye
on you. It's a feng shui thing."

they should practice seat rearrangement until they can move desks quickly and quietly. In addition, having students move to various locations in the room during instruction facilitates episodic memory because the brain not only remembers what it learns but also where it was when it learned it.

Because brains were meant to exist in the real world, the closer the classroom can approximate a homelike environment, the better. Some middle and high school classrooms have very little on the walls. Images on the walls can be very effective support for learning and give students something relevant to look at when their attention to direct instruction wanes. However, balance is necessary. Some elementary teachers have an excess of wall content. Too much on the wall can overstimulate students, especially students whose brains have difficulty focusing and paying attention.

Adding plants can help with needed oxygen. Family pictures on a teacher's desk enable students to realize that they are being taught by a real person with a life outside of the school day. Proactive managers plan their classroom environment so that students have an atmosphere most conducive to positive thinking and long-term retention.

WHY: THEORETICAL FRAMEWORK

In collaborative classrooms, students don't have desks or sit in rows because the whole classroom is a teaching tool where students interact with one another (Allen & Currie, 2012).

Changing room arrangement following a unit of study strengthens the episodic memory pathway, which attaches the student's learning to the context in which it was acquired (Tileston, 2004).

Where students are seated in the classroom and who they sit next to influences their stress levels, and stress in turn influences cognition (Jensen, 2007).

Walls should be used to teach and built by students around what they are learning at the time (Allen & Currie, 2012).

Considerations for room arrangement include the following:

- Can students move without running into each other?
- Are students close enough to the front of the room?
- Are students close enough to share the learning but far enough apart not to be distracting?
- Can the teacher easily circulate among student desks?
- Can all students see the teacher and the board?
- Do students have easy access to frequently used materials?
- Are there homelike touches in the room such as plants, lamps, and so on?
- Are visuals on the wall simple but related to the learning?
- Does computer placement facilitate a calm learning environment? (Smith, 2004)

When students work with partners or groups to complete an assignment, they should be allowed some flexibility in where they meet together as long as they are sitting at eye level with one another (Allen & Currie, 2012).

Students are not paying close attention to instruction when they are distracted by the shape or tilt of their desks or are consistently shifting in their uncomfortable chairs (Jensen, 2007).

Students' desks should be arranged so that the teacher can be seen during either whole-class or small-group instruction, but high-traffic areas should be kept clear (Wong & Wong, 1998).

HOW: CLASSROOM APPLICATION

- Arrange your classroom to provide some alternate forms of seating. Bring in an old sofa, a rocking chair, a beanbag chair, or carpet squares so that students can sit on the floor with a partner and complete an assignment.

- Rather than desks, request tables and chairs so that the strategy of reciprocal teaching or cooperative learning is facilitated. This type of seating makes it easier for students to talk with a partner or *family* of peers when necessary. It also provides writing or drawing space when completing a project or assignment.

- Place a podium or stand in the back of the classroom so that hyperactive children (or those who just need a break from sitting) can write and participate while standing.

- Teach students how to move their chairs into different configurations to facilitate various learning structures such as pairs for reciprocal teaching or groups of four or five to facilitate cooperative learning. This is known as *forming* and must be taught. Teach them how to move their desks back when the cooperative learning activity is over. Have them practice this ritual until it becomes habitual.

- Give students options in the classroom for where they would like to meet with their cooperative groups. This might include a table in the back of the room, a sofa, the counter, or the rug. Be sure that, as they talk, all students are at eye level with one another.

- Find reasons for students to add oxygen and blood to their brains simply by standing while learning. For example, they could be on their feet while discussing information or reteaching a concept to a peer. For another example, when teaching the difference between common and proper nouns, students could remain seated when a common noun is named and stand every time a proper noun is named.

- Have students change their episodic memory by changing their location in the room. If you are not comfortable with students constantly changing seats, then have them stand and review a concept just taught by moving to another area of the room.

- Find ways to engage students' bodies while learning. They could be role-playing an event in history or acting out a vocabulary word. There are multiple opportunities to engage both brain and body in the act of learning.

- In addition to flexible seating, give your classroom a more authentic, homey look by including live or artificial plants, an aquarium, pictures on the walls, and personal artifacts that symbolize your life. These could include pictures of your family, degrees earned, hobbies, and so on. As your students are a part of your school family, shouldn't your classroom look like their home?

REFLECTION

> ### What is my plan for incorporating alternative seating and natural artifacts into my classroom to make it more authentic?

_____

_____

_____

_____

_____

_____

_____

_____

_____

_____

_____

_____

_____

_____

_____

_____

_____

_____

DETOUR

Engage the Brains
of Your Students

9

Use Brain-Compatible Strategies

Your best defense against behavior problems is an engaging lesson.

Marcia L. Tate

WHAT: ENGAGING THE BRAIN

Research on the brain began more than 50 years ago when Dr. Roger Sperry attempted to control seizures in epileptic patients by severing the corpus callosum, the structure that joins the left and right hemispheres of the brain. These patients appeared to function normally but would use either the left or the right hemispheres of the brain depending on what the task required. We now realize that a left- and right-hemisphere theory of the brain is much too simplistic and that brains consistently use both hemispheres. For example, one's ability to appreciate music was once thought to be a right-hemisphere function. However, a classical pianist uses the organizational and structural functions of the left hemisphere as well.

Research on the brain continued into the 1990s, when millions of dollars were spent attempting to find cures for diseases such as Parkinson's and Alzheimer's. As a result, we know more today than ever before about how the brain works, even though there is a tremendous amount that we still do not know. For example, it appears that the frontal lobe of the brain does not fully mature until one is in his or her mid-20s, while the emotional part, or amygdala, matures much earlier. This is part of the reason that many of the decisions teenagers make are based on their emotions rather than what is logical.

For more than 25 years, I have read, studied, and researched about the brain and come to the conclusion that there are 20 ways to deliver instruction so that all students remember. Regardless of the learning style theory (Gardner, 1983; Sternberg & Grigorenko, 2000) you examine, the strategies are reflected. (See Table 9.1: Comparison of Brain-Compatible Instructional Strategies to Learning Theory at the end of this chapter for a list of the strategies and their correlation to learning style theory.) These strategies form the basis of the eight books I have written for administrators, teachers, and parents, so they too will know how to engage the brains of all learners. These strategies work for any age, any grade level, any content area, and any area of specialty including attention deficit disorder (ADD)/ ADHD, ESL, or autism. They not only increase academic achievement and make teaching and learning fun, but for the purposes of this book, they will definitely decrease your behavior problems. Remember, your best defense against classroom management problems is an engaging lesson.

When you see the list, you may notice that the strategies are used most often at the lower grades. It is in kindergarten that we sing, dance, and laugh to learn. As learners proceed to the upper grades, some educators have the mistaken assumption that the strategies are no longer needed. I am attempting to put a new paradigm in place that provides a rationale for why all learners, regardless of age, need to be taught in this way. Read on to find out why and how this chapter may be one of the most beneficial in the entire book.

WHY: THEORETICAL FRAMEWORK

A student may feel isolated when a teacher cannot connect with the way that student actually learns (Medina, 2008).

When hands-on activities are used, kinesthetic learners excel (Allen & Currie, 2012).

It can be very helpful for students to draw personally meaningful pictures when learning new vocabulary words and terms (Dean, Hubbell, Pitler, & Stone, 2012).

The chemical dopamine, which is released during the playing of a game, increases a student's ability to focus (Willis, 2007).

Since stress, anger, and fear shut down the brain's ability to learn; students learn best when their emotions are positive (Sousa & Tomlinson, 2011).

Participatory and advanced organizers present concepts in a way that enables students to link new knowledge to existing knowledge (Bender, 2012).

When students are made to sit quietly for long periods of time, recall and understanding are prohibited (Allen & Currie, 2012).

Changing the pace of instruction and giving students a choice of how they will show what they have learned can stimulate engagement. These choices can include multimedia or interactive projects, original dances, illustrations, musical renditions, and so forth (Cooper & Garner, 2012).

Our perception of the world is dominated by visual processing (Medina, 2008).

Positive visualizations create positive feelings because those visualizations release endorphins (Cooper & Garner, 2012).

HOW: CLASSROOM APPLICATION

- Because we remember 90 percent of what we talk about as we complete an activity (Ekwall & Shanker, 1988), student conversation should be an integral part of instruction. Have students reteach their partners a concept you have just taught them, debate a relevant issue, or engage in a *family* discussion regarding a controversial topic. See Chapter 11 for additional ways to integrate student talk into instructional activities.

- Many students in a classroom, especially boys, are visual, spatial learners, which may also make them excellent artists. Capitalize on this area of expertise by having students incorporate artwork across the curriculum. They could draw the meanings of a multiple-meaning word, the stages of mitosis, or the geographic features of a particular area of the world. Nonlinguistic representations, or drawings, simply make more sense to some brains when learning.

- Take students on a field trip to a location that connects the content being taught to the real world. Teachers often wait too long to take a field trip. Taking a trip earlier will make the learning more relevant and provide students with a real-world connection to the content. I still remember taking a field trip to the Young People's Concert, which the Atlanta Symphony sponsored when I was in elementary school. This annual event is one of the reasons that I still possess a love for all different types of music, including classical.

- Students learn best when the brain is not in high stress! Games and humor can lower the threat level when learning. Appoint a class clown to tell a joke or riddle at an appointed time or involve students in a spirited game of Jeopardy to review content prior to a test. These are both excellent ways to ensure that students look forward to showing up for class every day. Consult Chapter 13 for additional ways to incorporate lots of laughter in your classroom.

- One of the most powerful strategies on the list is that of metaphor, analogy, and simile. When students can relate a new concept to one that the student already knows, a memorable connection is made. For example, when teaching students a second language, any time the teacher says, *"This new word is like a word you already know,"* a neural connection is established.

- HOMES, PEMDAS, and FACE are all cross-curricular acronyms that assist students in recalling content. Any time you can create an acrostic or acronym that will help them remember, do so. However, if students are old enough, have them create their own mnemonic devices. The brain remembers best what it helps to create.

- One of the best ways to get students to remember anything is to incorporate movement into the learning. When students stand to read, talk to a partner, or agree with a peer, they send more blood and oxygen to the brain. When they role-play the steps in a word problem, an important event in American history, or the digestive process, students remember the content embedded in the role play. See Chapter 12 for additional ways to integrate movement into instructional practice.

• Engaging students in real-life projects not only ensures that content will be remembered but enables you to consolidate and teach a large numbers of objectives simultaneously. For example, have students create a Civil War newspaper as a project. Work with students to create a rubric that will be used to assess the newspaper. Each newspaper may include a title, a byline, a table of contents, a feature story with an image, an editorial, an ad, and a crime report. Not only will students demonstrate their comprehension of the Civil War, but they will also learn the function of the parts of a newspaper.

• Are you a great storyteller? You need to become one. History has been passed down for generations through the art of telling wonderful stories. However, do not tell stories for the sake of the art. You have no time for that! Create stories that enable students to understand the content you are teaching. When students recall your story, they will remember the content that the story was attempting to teach. You can even have students create their own stories to enable them to recall pertinent content.

• Work study not only reduces behavioral infractions but also makes content extremely relevant to all brains. For example, when students are placed in alternative education due to their inability to be successful in a regular school setting, they are often involved in work study or on-the-job training. Career academies and High Schools That Work programs also take advantage of the fact that students learn to do real jobs by doing real jobs. Apprenticeships, internships, practica, and student teaching are all viable and effective ways to help students comprehend and retain knowledge and skill. Assign students to experts in a field who can involve them in a work-study experience related to course content. Then step back, and watch them learn!

• Writing is often viewed as a laborious practice where a piece of creativity is carried through several stages of an arduous process. While that certainly is writing, it is not the only way students can show what they know through the written word. Have students do *quick writes* to recall cross-curricular content. For example, a teacher could have students write down all the critical attributes of a *triangle* in less than 2 minutes. By the way, it appears that writing in longhand is more memorable to the brain than typing on a computer.

Table 9.1 Comparison of Brain-Compatible Instructional Strategies to Learning Theory

Brain-Compatible Strategies	Multiple Intelligences	Visual, Auditory, Kinesthetic, or Tactile (VAKT)
Brainstorming and discussion	Verbal–linguistic	Auditory
Drawing and artwork	Spatial	Kinesthetic and tactile
Field trips	Naturalist	Kinesthetic and tactile
Games	Interpersonal	Kinesthetic and tactile
Graphic organizers, semantic maps, and word webs	Logical–mathematical/ spatial	Visual and tactile
Humor	Verbal–linguistic	Auditory
Manipulatives, experiments, labs, and models	Logical–mathematical	Tactile
Metaphors, analogies, and similes	Spatial	Visual and auditory
Mnemonic devices	Musical–rhythmic	Visual and auditory
Movement	Bodily–kinesthetic	Kinesthetic
Music, rhythm, rhyme, and rap	Musical–rhythmic	Auditory
Project-based and problem-based learning	Logical–mathematical	Visual and tactile
Reciprocal teaching and cooperative learning	Verbal–linguistic	Auditory
Role plays, drama, pantomimes, charades	Bodily–kinesthetic	Kinesthetic
Storytelling	Verbal–linguistic	Auditory
Technology	Spatial	Visual and tactile
Visualization and guided imagery	Spatial	Visual
Visuals	Spatial	Visual
Work study and apprenticeships	Interpersonal	Kinesthetic
Writing and journals	Intrapersonal	Visual and tactile

REFLECTION

What is my plan for incorporating brain-compatible strategies into my instructional delivery?

_____

_____

_____

_____

_____

_____

_____

_____

_____

_____

_____

_____

_____

_____

_____

_____

_____

_____

_____

_____

10
Hook Them Into Relevant Lessons

"Control may get you compliance, creating connections gets you the commitment."

Jabari, 2013

WHAT: ATTENTION AND THE BRAIN

You might think that, when students are sitting quietly and looking at you, you have their undivided attention. Let me tell you something you probably have already figured out. Students can be looking dead in your face and not paying a bit of attention to what you are saying. Just because you have their eyes doesn't mean that you have their brains. In fact, the average attention span for listening to a lecture is commensurate with the age of the student. For example, a 6-year-old appears able to listen without active engagement for about 6 minutes, a 12-year-old 12 minutes, and so forth. However, the maximum amount of time, even for an adult, is approximately 20 minutes. After that time, without active engagement, the brain has simply had enough (Tileston, 2004).

Even within the aforementioned time parameters, teachers stand a better chance of capturing students' attention if they utilize any one of four *hooks* for the brain: need, novelty, meaning, or emotion. In fact, behavior problems are minimized when teachers have the full attention of students during a lesson. Television and movie producers know the power of the *hook*. How many times have you been watching a show or a movie in which something occurred during the first few minutes to hook your attention? For example, the second-longest-running television drama in history, *Law and Order,* always hooked you by showing the crime in the first few minutes. During some seasons of the show *Seinfeld,* Jerry Seinfeld opened with a stand-up comedy routine related to the topic of the show. Steven Spielberg opened the movie *Jaws* with a horrific scene in which a woman swimming alone is attacked and killed by a great white shark.

Teachers are also entertainers whose job is to capture the interest of their audience. What better way to do that than with the four engagement hooks: *need, novelty, meaning,* and *emotion.* Let's consider each one separately.

Need

Have you ever learned something because you simply needed to know it? Need is a useful way of getting and keeping the brain's attention. People learn what they need to know when they need to know it. Most human beings today don't even see the need to memorize telephone numbers if those numbers can be programmed into their cell phones. They will memorize a number when the information cannot be retrieved any other way. Convince students that they need the information you are teaching, and they will more than likely pay attention to it.

To establish students' need for what you are teaching, give them a purpose for learning it. Open your lesson with a reason why the particular objective you are teaching is necessary to master. For example, if I am teaching students a lesson on cause and effect, I tell them that everything that happens in life appears to have a cause and every cause tends to have an effect. I explain that, if you are aware of the causes and effects of events, then you can predict what may occur.

Simply telling students that they need to remember content for a test is an insufficient purpose for many students. They are not motivated to do well just because you want high test scores. Sometimes, teachers will tell me that they truly cannot think of a reason why students need to know what they are teaching. You know what my next question to them is. Then why teach it?

Novelty

If need will not work for your lesson, the next hook is novelty. The brain also pays attention to things that are new or different. Novelty is a motivator that can be easily incorporated into a teacher's lessons. Let me tell you a short story. (There I go using one of the 20 strategies that take advantage of the way brains learn best: storytelling.)

For 17 years, I lived in a subdivision across the street from a railroad track. When we first moved in, I could hear the train every time it came down the track. That lasted less than a month. Soon, the noise of the train was not novel anymore, and I rarely paid any attention to the train's scheduled runs. This story is analogous to what happens in a classroom when students come to expect lessons presented in the same way day after day—through boring lectures or numerous worksheets. Soon they, too, are not paying attention anymore.

Why not add a little novelty into your lessons each day so that students never know exactly what to expect in your lesson presentation? In fact, while your classroom rituals and procedures should remain constant, your lesson should not. The brain-compatible strategies outlined in Chapter 9 of this book should serve as vehicles for a never-ending supply of novelty. For example, I teach nine different professional development classes. Each one is novel. I use different music, games, stories, and so on to maintain the interest of those teachers who have taken several different classes from me. Just visualize how many different stories you can tell, movements or role plays that your students can perform, songs you can sing, or projects in which your students can engage. While there are only 20 strategies, there are an unlimited number of ways to utilize them.

Meaning

A third way to gain students' attention is to connect the learning to real life. It stands to reason that, if the brain was meant to survive in the real world, then the closer a teacher can get the instruction to the real world, the more memorable it becomes. Here's a real-life example. My daughter Jessica had been studying German in college and learned a great deal from the classes she took. However, it was not until she spent a summer interning and living in Germany and taking courses at the University of Berlin that she really began to apply and internalize what she had been learning in that artificial place called school.

For a primary classroom, counting money doesn't mean anything until we set up a classroom store and buy and sell goods that cost the amounts that students are trying to learn. Percentages don't mean a thing until you tell students that, after today's lesson, they will be able to approximate how much money they can save when they see a percent-off sign on any item in the store. One high school math teacher told me that his students did not understand logarithms until the Japanese earthquake happened and he realized that the Richter scale is a logarithmic scale. When students can see the connection between what you are teaching and their world, attention is increased. However, you have to know something about your students' lives to appropriately connect what you are teaching to their world.

Emotion

The final motivator for capturing attention is emotion. Of all four, it is possibly the most powerful. Anything that happened in the world or in your personal life that was filled with emotion tends to be unforgettable. I bet you can even remember what you were doing on January 28, 1986, when you heard that the *Challenger* shuttle had exploded in space. Even though that was more than 25 years ago, most people have no difficulty recalling where they were because that day was filled with emotion. After all, even a teacher was on board.

However, I do not want to use a negative definition of emotion when talking about teaching and learning. If you were ever in the classroom of a teacher you did not like, you will never forget being in his or her room, but you will not remember the content. Your brain was in survival mode, and when the brain is under threat, memory is compromised. Teaching with a passion or love for your content also emotionally connects you with students and students to the lesson. Do you remember teachers who were so enthusiastic about their content that their enthusiasm became contagious—a math teacher who made you love math or a science teacher who instilled in you a curiosity about the world? Emotion, then, becomes a powerful motivator.

What about the flip side of emotion? What about the students who enter your room daily with brains in such a state of high stress that they cannot think? While you may be able to do little to reduce the stresses of your students' personal lives, your classroom might be the one bright spot in their otherwise dismal day. Make your classroom a positive place to be emotionally, and the learning will follow. While low to moderate stress can be good for learning, the brain learns best when it is not in high stress!

WHY: THEORETICAL FRAMEWORK

Relevance stimulates students to be cognitively engaged as it encourages them to bring something to the learning experience (Cooper & Garner, 2012).

If content is irrelevant to the brain, an existing neuron will not connect to another neuron nearby (Jensen, 2008).

When teachers use concrete examples from students' lives, relational memories are created (Willis, 2007).

Much of what is taught in classrooms does not have the personal relevance essential for learning authentically (Jensen, 2008).

Information is more firmly woven into the brain when a great number of links, associations, or connections are created (Jensen, 2008).

"Control may get you compliance, creating connections gets you the commitment" (Jabari, 2013, p. 74).

The brain likes novelty because whatever the brain perceives as unusual wakes it up and causes it to produce norepinephrine (Sprenger, 2005).

Without novelty, students can become bored and passive and may resort to engaging in other things such as doodling, talking to peers, daydreaming, or misbehaving (Cooper & Garner, 2012).

Two mechanisms built into the human brain that help students pay attention to content are the need for change and novelty and the need for information packed with emotion (Jensen, 2007).

"Logic moves the mind; emotion moves the body" (Jabari, 2013, p. 73).

HOW: CLASSROOM APPLICATION

- Your students' brains are motivated by information that is needed to survive in the real world. Open your lesson by telling students what they will be learning and why they need the information or skill you will be teaching. For example, when teaching students how to calculate simple interest, tell them that they need this skill so that they will be able to transact a loan for a future car.

- The brain pays attention to things that are novel, new, or different. Keep novelty alive in the classroom by changing things in the environment such as rearranging student desks, bringing in plants, or introducing different types of music in support of the lesson.

- Dressing in a novel way, moving around the room, or changing the pace of the class or the tone of your voice are other ways to maintain students' attention (Feinstein, 2004).

- Changing students' locations in the room is a way to give them a fresh and different perspective. In fact, simply having students learn something in one location in the room and review it while sitting in a different location places the information at two different sites in the brain, enabling students to recall it from either place.

- The best way to keep novelty alive in the classroom is to vary instruction using the brain-compatible strategies outlined in Chapter 9. While it is important to maintain consistent classroom rituals and procedures, it is equally important to use a variety of methods for delivering instruction. This way, students come to class excited because they never know what to expect. For example, when teaching vocabulary, have students role-play the definition, illustrate the meaning, visualize the word connected to its definition, or write a song that symbolizes the concept.

- Relevance is a key component in understanding and retention. When students can see the connection between what they are learning and their world, retention improves. Therefore, always use real-life examples to illustrate points being made in a lesson. For example, when teaching students to solve word problems, I never begin with the problems in the math text. I use the names of students in the class and make up original problems based on actual events in their lives. For example, when teaching a lesson that helped students solve word problems by setting up an algebraic equation, I asked Jocelyn, Jamar, and Camry about a trip to the movies and set the equation up involving the outing.

- Emotion is an important way that the brain stores information. Anything emotional that happened in your personal life or in the world at large is long remembered. For example, in the opening of one lesson on the Holocaust, show poignant scenes from *Schindler's List*. In another lesson, don't tell students what concept you are teaching, but make alarming statements about teenagers as soon as they get in the classroom. When students are really upset, announce that they have just experienced the negative effects of *propaganda*. You'll have their attention.

- Teach your content with enthusiasm. Show passion and love for the subject you teach, and that passion will become contagious. There is nothing better for maintaining the attention of students than an interesting lesson taught by a motivated teacher. After all, one of the major reasons students disrupt is boredom.

REFLECTION

> **What is my plan for gaining and maintaining students' attention in a lesson?**

_____

_____

_____

_____

_____

_____

_____

_____

_____

_____

_____

_____

_____

_____

_____

_____

_____

_____

11

Let Them Talk!

The person doing the most talking about the content is growing the most brain cells.

Marcia L. Tate

WHAT: CONVERSATION AND THE BRAIN

As rhymes are brain compatible, I wrote an original one to symbolize what we teachers and administrators do to students in schools. It is as follows:

Students can't talk in class.

They can't talk in the hall.

They can't talk in the cafeteria.

They can't talk at all!

Did you like my original effort? If the brain is a social organism, then why are students' brains not allowed to socialize in class to learn what they need to know? I will never forget my sixth-grade math teacher, Mr. Mitchell, who did not allow us to talk, ever! Even when he was out of the room, he appointed a class monitor who wrote down the names of any student who talked. Anyone whose name appeared on the list was required to stay after school. When he returned to class, if he heard any noise at all or was having a bad day, he kept the entire class after school. What good did it do me to behave if I was going to be kept after school anyway? I made up my mind right then and there that, when I became a teacher, I would never keep the entire class after school for what a few students were doing. And I never did! I now know, however, that talking in class should never have been deemed misbehavior. In fact, one of the best things a student can do is *talk back to you!* Teachers should be asking questions and students supplying answers as much as possible. Unless students respond orally, how will you know that they are with you?

The neuroscientists are telling us that the person in the classroom who is doing the most talking is growing the most dendrites (brain cells). Why is this the case? Let's consider two reasons. First, when a person opens his or her mouth to speak, that action sends oxygen to the brain, which wakes the brain up and makes it more alert. How alert have you been after sitting in a boring staff development class for a half or full day? Because the brain does not wish to be bored, teachers often bring papers to grade, texts to send, or even work to do so that, even in the most boring of circumstances, the brain is at least occupied.

Oxygen is essential to the brain. In fact, if a brain is deprived of oxygen for 3 to 4 minutes, one is literally brain dead. I have been in some classrooms, particularly in middle and high school, where students were breathing, but it was difficult to tell. They were figuratively brain dead.

In classrooms that are truly brain compatible, students don't have time to be bored because one of the things that engages their brains is excessive talking. In fact, they should be talking at least twice as much as the teacher. This feat is easier to accomplish than you might expect. An example follows: When you begin a new lesson, often you will be talking to your students, telling them what they need to know. However, when you review the information, you should be asking the questions, and the class should be providing the answers as choral responses. For example, when I teach classes about the physiology of the brain, I ask review questions like the following and have the class provide the answers in a strong, loud, choral response: *How much does the brain weigh? (3 pounds); What is the name of the structure over which the two hemispheres talk? (the corpus callosum).* Not only does this activity engage students, but it gives me a pretty good indication of what my class truly remembers of what I just taught them.

When I am pretty sure that students know what they are talking about, I have them talk with a partner, which leads us to the second reason that students should be talking: The brain learns 90 percent of what it teaches to another brain (Society for Developmental Education, 1995; Sousa, 2006). Teach your students, and then have them reteach what you just taught to a partner. You would be surprised how that simple activity enables both partners (teacher and learner) to retain the information.

Many students get in trouble in class for doing the very thing that comes naturally to the brain: talking. Let them talk—aloud to you and then to a partner. By the time the information has been bantered about three times, most brains will have it. Use the brains of other students to help you teach content. In my classes, there is the following rule: Ask three, then me. If students have a question about what you are teaching, they should ask three peers prior to asking you.

Teachers often ask me this question: *What if they talk about something else when they are supposed to be discussing the course content?* This is what I tell them. I give my students permission to talk about whatever they want, provided they have discussed the assignment first and are ready to respond should I call on them. The routine is called *My Stuff, Your Stuff!* The simple act of telling them that what they have to say is important alleviates a great deal of the sneaking around and off-task behavior that gets so many students in trouble.

By the way, I have been teaching teachers and administrators for more than 20 years. Teachers are some of the chattiest people I know. Isn't it ironic that people who love to talk will often not allow students to participate in the same activity?

WHY: THEORETICAL FRAMEWORK

"When students toss around a variety of ideas and express their opinions, they can *increase the amount of paper manipulated and stored into the filing cabinet* of the brain, slowly forming a more complex outlook on the topic" (Allen & Currie, 2012, p. 41).

The quiet classroom where students are raising their hands to speak out is not congruent with the way many diverse cultures communicate (B. M. Davis, 2006).

Student engagement is increased, affective filters lowered, and student participation invited when teachers use successful student-centered question-and-response discussions (Willis, 2007).

Students can be assisted in mastering concepts when paired discussion, partner-based activities, paired timed tests, and so forth are used following initial teaching (Marzano & Pickering, 2011).

Having students talk about new information with their peers is one of the most powerful ways for them to process it (Allen & Currie, 2012).

Students can receive special recognition for their original thoughts when teachers give them opportunities to brainstorm (Armstrong, 2009).

Following an actual experience, having students verbally retell ideas and events through dialogue and discussion helps the brain tap into cognitive memory (Fogarty, 2009).

Not allowing students to talk decreases the likelihood that any new material will be processed and embedded into long-term memory (Hattie, 2009).

Rather than striving for continued focus or complete silence, teachers should build in collaborative or talk time for students (Crawford, 2004).

When same-sex companions were separated from their peers and not allowed to talk to them, they showed a dramatic increase in cortisol (the stress hormone) levels from 18 to 87 percent (Levine, Baukol, & Pavlidis, 1999).

HOW: CLASSROOM APPLICATION

• When students come into your class, allow them to talk quietly until they begin a sponge activity or until you start the daily lesson. If you have some type of calming music playing (such as classical, jazz, or new age), you can encourage them to talk beneath the sound of the music. In fact, tell them that if you can hear their individual voices over the music, then they are talking too loudly.

• Teach students a routine called *My Turn, Your Turn.* The ritual is used to remind students that it is important that, when it is the teacher's turn to talk, all attention must be focused on the teacher as the brain can only pay conscious attention to one thing at a time. Then, the teacher will provide time for students to talk with one another.

• After you have taught a segment of content, stop and ask questions of the entire class to ascertain whether they have understood and retained the information just taught. Encourage everyone in the class to answer your questions in loud, strong, choral responses. You may even have them stand up in an effort to send more blood and oxygen to the brain while they are answering your designated questions and reviewing content.

• The brain needs specific feedback if it is to understand exactly what behavior is expected of it. When students talk with one another, give them feedback as to the noise level you expect. For example, Jeff Battle, a seventh-grade teacher in Tennessee, has the following five voice levels in his classroom:

  ○ 0—Quiet of the tomb
  ○ 1—*Double-O* spy talk
  ○ 2—Low flow
  ○ 3—Formal normal
  ○ 4—Loud crowd
  ○ 5—Out of control

He has students practice the voice levels until they become second nature.

• When you need students' attention, you need it at a moment's notice, and you should not have to scream or yell over their talking to get it. After all, *Shouting Won't Grow Dendrites!* Devise a signal for getting students' attention. It can be as simple as a raised hand, the ringing of chimes, or the clapping of hands. It doesn't matter what signal you use as long as you have one. Teach the signal to your students on the first day of school, and reinforce it throughout the year. In fact, brains get tired of the same signal all of the time, so vary your attention getters.

• Have students select close partners; a close partner is someone in the class who sits so close that the pair can talk without getting out of their seats. Have students talk to their close partners whenever time is limited and you need students to reteach information just taught, brainstorm ideas, or review pertinent content prior to a test. Close partners can also be used to re-explain something when it is not easily understood.

- Place students in cooperative groups or families of three to five members. Assign these families tasks to complete related to the lesson you are teaching. For example, families can discuss what they know about a given topic or be given specific discussion questions to get them talking. When I taught a model lesson recently in an alternative school, many students were almost asleep or disengaged when I entered the room. However, as the assignment had been to read the book *The Giver,* each student was soon engaged in a discussion of the following question: Is there really such a thing as utopia? You could immediately see the change in student demeanor when they began talking about a subject of interest.

- Engage the entire class in brainstorming or discussing ideas related to a selected topic. Brainstorming and discussion not only get students talking, but this strategy also assists students' brains in activating prior knowledge. Be certain to ask questions at the following higher levels of Bloom's Taxonomy—comprehension, application, analysis, synthesis, and evaluation.

- Have students generate their own questions to ask peers regarding course content or a reading selection. Students are more motivated when answering their own queries rather than those provided by the teacher or textbook (National Reading Panel, 2000).

REFLECTION

> What is my plan for incorporating appropriate
> *talk* time into my classroom?

_____

_____

_____

_____

_____

What activities will I use that enable students to talk with their peers about content?

_____

_____

_____

_____

_____

What rituals will I use to signal the beginning and ending of talk time for students?

_____

_____

_____

_____

_____

_____

12

Let Them Move!

Tell me; I forget! Show me; I remember! Involve me; I understand.

Old Chinese Proverb

WHAT: MOVEMENT AND THE BRAIN

It is 8:55 a.m.—time to change classes in Washington High School. Students are relieved because they get to actually move their bodies to the next location. However, in most middle or high schools, that is probably the last time they will get to move for the next 55 minutes or until the bell rings for the next period. In fact, if any student attempts to move during the period, that student is in trouble for being out of his or her seat.

If the purpose of school is to prepare students for success in the world of work, what job in the real world can you think of where the employee is not allowed to move? Even if a person has a desk job, I doubt that the boss stands over him or her and forbids him or her to get out of the desk chair.

Consider this. There are some things that you know how to do that you will never forget how to do, even if you live to be 100 (e.g., driving a car, riding a bicycle, typing, playing the piano). You remember these activities because you were moving when you learned them, which meant that the information was placed in one of the strongest memory systems in the brain: procedural or muscle memory. One teacher related to me that her mother has Alzheimer's and cannot recognize her own daughter or her grandchildren. However, her mother is a pianist. Her mother can still go to the piano and play songs that she once played.

Here is another story told to me by a teacher in one of my classes. She told me about her grandmother, who was in the hospital in a coma. Her grandmother had knitted all of her life. She is now lying in her hospital bed going through the motion of knitting—no needle, no thread, but still knitting! The teacher walked up to the bed and told her grandmother that she could stop knitting because the piece was finished. Within minutes, her grandmother stopped *knitting* and passed away!

Procedural memory is accessed when students are actively engaged in the learning process. If you have ever taken a computer course, you know that, unless you placed your hands on the keyboard during the course and then continued to practice what you learned, your brain did not retain the new skill. Having students dance the number line hustle to add positive and negative integers, role-play vocabulary words to retain their meaning, or conduct an experiment to draw conclusions regarding a given hypothesis will go a long way toward ensuring that they will not only retain the concepts being taught but also have fun in the process.

A football coach in Wiley, Texas, stated in my workshop that procedural memory explains why the football players who cannot retain their content long enough to pass their content-area tests can remember every play on the field. I told the coach that, while he is running the plays, football players in other classes are just sitting still.

Movement also has a therapeutic effect on the brain and body. This is why people usually feel so much better after they walk, swim, or engage in other forms of exercise. Getting students kinesthetically involved in a lesson or walking a student down the hall when he or she is angry tends to calm that student's brain down (Jensen, 2000b; Thayer, 1996).

During a few of my after-school workshops, I have noticed that some teachers are not in the best frame of mind when they arrive because they have been required to attend. Chances are they have never been in one of my workshops and have expectations of inactivity and boredom. The sooner I get them up and moving, the faster I see the state of their brain change from negative to positive. Why is this? In the brain, there are positive and negative chemicals called neurotransmitters. Some of the positive ones are produced when people are moving—chemicals like endorphins, dopamine, and serotonin. These can be very beneficial for students because they not only assist them in remembering content, but they also contribute to the joy of learning.

WHY: THEORETICAL FRAMEWORK

Because physical exercise increases levels of serotonin, dopamine, and norepinephrine, children and adolescents are in the best state for learning following exercise (Nevills, 2011).

When used carefully and with a purpose, controlled movement can actually result in a more disciplined and productive classroom (Lengel & Kuczala, 2010).

Teenagers improve their cognitive processing skills as physical movement helps their cerebellums develop (Feinstein, 2009).

Having students working quietly at their desks eliminates the up to 40 percent of kinesthetic learners who have to be moving to learn (Hattie, 2009).

The neural connections in an adolescent's cerebellum are strengthened when that adolescent is involved in bodily kinesthetic movement, such as physical education classes or extracurricular activities (Feinstein, 2004).

Studies of the impact of movement and exercise on 18,600 students in Naperville District 203 near Chicago led guidance counselors to recommend that all students take their most challenging academic classes immediately after physical education (Dibble, 2008).

Physical performance is probably the only known cognitive activity that uses 100 percent of the brain (Jensen, 2008).

Combining kinesthetic activities with curriculum content has been shown to increase the test scores of elementary students (Madigan & Hess, 2006).

When movement is added to learning, it activates those crucial regions in the frontal lobe that are not as developed in ADHD students (Willis, 2007).

Learners with special needs are helped by movement in the following ways: (1) It changes their states, (2) it activates a wide variety of areas in the brain, and (3) it increases the energy levels and blood flow or calms those who are overactive (Jensen, 2005a).

Movement is the door to learning (Dennison, 1990).

HOW: CLASSROOM APPLICATION

• As content is discussed, have students stand if they agree with a statement and remain seated if they disagree with it. This simple procedure actively engages both brain and body and can prevent behavior problems.

• When there is something that must be read aloud, have specific groups of students or the entire class stand and read the assigned material aloud. Simply having students stand will wake them up and make them more alert.

• Have students draw a clock with the following four times on it: 12:00, 3:00, 6:00, and 9:00. Have them draw one line near each time. Then, they walk around the room to music and make one appointment with each of four different classmates who sit at a distance from them. After students have been sitting for a while, have them stand and move to one of the classmates they made an appointment with to discuss an assigned topic.

Just standing and walking will add more blood and oxygen to the brain and facilitate learning.

- Have students make a seasonal appointment with four peers who sit at a distance from them. They will make a summer, fall, winter, and spring appointment with four different students as you assign specific information that needs to be discussed or tasks that need to be completed. When you need to integrate movement into your lesson, have students keep one of their appointments.

- A wonderful review activity happens when fast-paced music is played and students are asked to stand and walk around the room to the beat of the high-energy music. Stop the music periodically and have students turn to a peer and answer a designated question regarding the content. Then, restart the music and repeat the procedure. Each time the music stops, a student should be talking to a different student. Continue until either all content has been reviewed or the song has ended.

- Have students role-play cross-curricular vocabulary or concepts. For example, in a mathematics class, have them use their arms to make obtuse, acute, and right angles. In a language arts class, have them act out the definitions of literary terms or reading vocabulary. These terms will be long remembered.

- Body spelling enables students to associate movement with the letters in words. For example, to spell the word *play,* students would bend toward the floor for the *p* and the *y* because those letters drop below the line. Students would spread their arms out to the side for the *a* in *play* because that letter remains on the line, and students would raise their arms toward the sky for the *1* because that letter extends above the line. Once students get the hang of it, they will be body spelling words like *photosynthesis* or *antiestablishment.*

- Play games with students to teach or reinforce content. Most games require some type of movement. Competing in a Jeopardy game while standing in teams, tossing a ball as students provide answers while reviewing for a test, and conducting a scavenger hunt to find hidden clues around the school are all examples of games that not only require movement but also produce lots of laughter.

- Involve students in activities that engage the brain in solving real-world problems or completing real-life projects. Designate a number of objectives that can be met through one project, and have students work individually or in teams to complete it. Project- and problem-based instruction pays big dividends toward understanding and retention.

• When students have been working intently for a long period of time, provide them with a stretch break. Have them stand and stretch their bodies to music as they make an effort to relax. This will give their brains a few minutes of much-needed downtime.

• Consult the text *Worksheets Don't Grow Dendrites: 20 Instructional Strategies That Engage the Brain* (2nd ed.) for more than 150 ways to actively engage student brains in learning. You will find that the more actively involved students are, the less you will have to deal with the major causes of misbehavior: boredom, attention, control, and inadequacy.

REFLECTION

> ### What is my plan for incorporating *movement* into my lessons?

What activities will I use that enable students to move as they are learning?

Objective or Standard:

_____

_____

Movement Activity:

_____

_____

Objective or Standard:

_____

_____

Movement Activity:

_____

_____

Objective or Standard:

_____

_____

Movement Activity:

_____

_____

What rituals will I use to signal the beginning and end of movement activities?

_____

_____

_____

_____

13

Keep Them Laughing

What we learn with pleasure, we never forget.

Allen, 2008

WHAT: HUMOR AND THE BRAIN

A cartoon was shown of a classroom where students were literally hanging from the ceiling, tied by their feet. Outside the door, there was a sign that read *In-School Suspension.* This cartoon shown in a workshop on classroom management practically ensures a chuckle or two. That chuckle goes a long way in creating a climate conducive for learning. Tempers can be cooled and showdowns often avoided when a teacher employs the age-old strategy of humor.

Laughter has been called *internal jogging* because it can have as beneficial an effect on the brain and body as traditional jogging and aerobic exercise. When students are learning content by participating in motivating simulations, when there is *feel-good* music playing in the background, and when students are *jogging internally,* the positive environment so essential for retention of information is created.

Humor can also result from students' involvement with games. I play Jeopardy with students and adults to review course content. They work in teams with a spokesperson who selects answers from various categories connected to the content being reviewed. The team then works together to provide the appropriate questions to the answers on the board, much the same way as contestants do during the television show. I even have the music for Jeopardy, which I play throughout the game show, and I call myself Alicia Trebek, the female counterpart to Alex. Students love it and laugh the entire time. Other games such as ball toss, *Wheel of Fortune,* and *Who Wants to Be a Millionaire* add excitement to what could be an otherwise boring lesson.

Eric Jensen (1998) suggests that middle or high school teachers appoint a class clown whose job it is to tell a riddle, pun, or joke at an appropriate time. (This activity is outlined in another section of this chapter.) After the class has worked hard and when their brains need some downtime, have the student tell the joke. Students will laugh, thereby facilitating memory and creating a positive classroom climate conducive to learning.

Don't ever confuse humor with sarcasm. Any statement that demeans or dehumanizes a student destroys the emotional support that so many students come to school needing. I have often heard teachers say, "When I am sarcastic, my students like it. They understand me, and they even laugh!" Ask yourself this question: What else are they going to do? Students have to save face in front of their peers, so even if they feel humiliated, they may not admit it to you. Then, consider this scenario. When the teacher says something sarcastic to a student, what if that student comes back with a sarcastic statement to the teacher? That student will probably be ordered out of class and to the office or, at the very least, reprimanded for disrespectful behavior. If you expect respect from your students, you must model it with your students.

WHY: THEORETICAL FRAMEWORK

It is possible for learning to be both rigorous and enjoyable (Cooper & Garner, 2012).

Humor and music are prime ingredients for improving students' emotional states, and that emotional climate has so much to do with how much students can learn (Lengel & Kuczala, 2010).

Because the language skills of older adolescents are more highly developed, they can understand the subtlety of humor, irony, or satire (Feinstein, 2009).

The production of endorphins, an increase in oxygen, and a decrease in pulse rate are three positive physiological effects of laughter (Costa, 2008).

The creative use of humor can engage students by making the content come alive, focus students' attention, increase retention, and relieve stress (Cooper & Garner, 2012).

When the teacher projects a positive and enthusiastic demeanor, students are likely to adopt the same attitude (Gettinger & Kohler, 2006).

A smile can cause students to straighten their posture, brighten their eyes, quicken their steps, and turn their frowns into smiles (Allen & Currie, 2012).

Optimism, the expectation that things will ultimately be all right, protects students from lapsing into hopelessness or depression when things are tough (Tileston, 2004).

Laughter can lighten the load, help students cope with stress, break up boredom, shorten the school day, and lengthen one's life (Burgess, 2000).

If people are to be motivated effectively, their needs for survival, love and belonging, power, freedom, and fun must be met (Glasser, 1999).

HOW: CLASSROOM APPLICATION

- Buy a joke book, and start your class with a joke of the day. If you tell a joke at the beginning of each period and students begin to look forward to it, they will be sure to show up on time for your class. After all, who wants to miss out on an opportunity to laugh?

- The brains of most students in the primary grades are not highly developed enough to understand the subtleties of jokes. But they love riddles. Here are some riddles to get you started:

  o *Why did the turtle cross the road? (to get to the shell station)*
  o *Where do bumblebees go to the bathroom? (at the BP station)*
  o *What did one strawberry say to the other strawberry? (if you weren't so fresh, we wouldn't be in this jam)*
  o *Why don't the circus lions eat the circus clowns? (because they taste funny)*

- Appoint a *class clown* whose job it is to tell a joke at an appointed time during the day or period. Have the student tell you the joke prior to class to make sure that it is appropriate for students. Jokes can put students' brains in the right frame of mind for learning and contribute to a positive classroom environment (Jensen, 1998).

"I am very proud to hear that my son is the class clown."

- Have students place appropriate jokes or riddles on cards and bring them to class. Read all jokes and riddles ahead of time for their appropriateness. Put all of the cards in a box, and have a student draw one card out daily. Share the joke with the entire class.

- Find cartoons that can accompany the content that you are teaching, and share them with the class at the appropriate time.

- Find a joke or cartoon, and read it aloud or show it to the class, omitting the punch line. Have students work on their inference skills by attempting to supply the missing punch line.

- As a sponge (warm-up) activity, have a riddle on the board when students arrive for class. Students may work individually or in teams to attempt to solve the riddle. They may turn their answers in on paper, and at the end of the class period or the week, the answer is revealed. Riddles not only provide fun and challenge but encourage higher-level thinking and reasoning.

- Have students bring in editorial cartoons to share with classmates. Encourage them to use their higher-level thinking skills to explain the reasoning behind the design of the cartoons.

- Have students create their own content-area jokes or riddles. For example, one middle school math student thought of this original riddle: *Why would you never say the number 288 in front of anyone?* Give up? The answer is: *It is just too gross (two gross).*

- Have students design their own cartoons, comic books, or superheroes to illustrate key concepts taught. For example, in science class, students could design a comic book in which the main character is Molecule Man, a superhero with all the strengths and powers of a molecule.

- Play games to review content prior to a test. When many brains hear the words *Let's play a game!*, the threat level in class goes down, and the retention level goes up as brains say, *"Oh, goody!"*

- Appreciate the creativity and comical lengths certain students go to in order to entertain themselves. Do as one teacher did. Keep a journal of all the weird and funny things students do in order to get attention in your classroom. When you take a step backward, you will begin to appreciate how truly creative students can be (Kottler, 2002).

REFLECTION

What is my plan for incorporating humor into my classroom?

List below the punch lines of jokes or the answers to riddles that you would like to incorporate.

_____

_____

_____

_____

_____

_____

_____

_____

_____

_____

_____

_____

_____

_____

_____

_____

_____

_____

DETOUR →

Develop a Proactive
Management Plan

14

Teach Your Rituals

The more procedures and practices are used,
the sooner they become habits.

Sprenger, 2003

WHAT: ESTABLISHING YOUR PROCEDURES

I was observing in a classroom in which the teacher had given students specific directions not to disturb her while she was conducting a guided reading group at the back table. Students were also instructed not to talk to their classmates while completing the seatwork that had been assigned. One student raised his hand and asked, "Mrs. Williams, what are we supposed to do if we have a question about our worksheet?" The teacher replied, "How many times have I told you that, if you have a question, ask your neighbor?"

What is wrong with this picture? Was this teacher sending mixed messages? If the class was not supposed to talk, how can this student ask a neighbor if he has a question? As a matter of fact, if the student who raised his hand had asked another student for help, he would now be in trouble for talking.

In every school, there are teachers who very effectively manage students. At first, it was thought that those teachers had some big bag of tricks that other teachers didn't have, which helped them to know just what to do in various situations. What the research is telling us is that effective classroom managers spend an inordinate amount of their time during the first few days and weeks of school establishing their expectations and procedures, in other words, their rituals (Wong & Wong, 1998). They teach all students the specific behaviors expected of them in any classroom situation. These situations include when and how to enter and leave the class, when to talk and how loudly, how to give you their undivided attention when you need it, when and how to distribute papers and how to turn in homework, what to do when absent from school, how to move around the classroom when warranted, and how to return to their seats when an activity is over.

"I replaced the clerk's bell with this gong.
Now I have no problem getting the attention
of all my students."

Effective classroom managers anticipate every part of the school day and determine a specific plan to help students successfully navigate through each part. They then teach these rituals to their students in much the same way they teach their content. Students practice, practice, practice until they follow the rituals habitually and to the satisfaction of the teacher. Effective teachers provide feedback after each practice and celebrate when students get it right. They then spend more time thanking those students who are appropriately practicing the rituals than reprimanding those students who are not.

WHY: THEORETICAL FRAMEWORK

Routines, or rituals, enable the classroom to function smoothly because they provide students with a sense of security over their classroom time and students know exactly what to expect (Pinto, 2013).

Teachers should introduce predictable routines that can drive their classroom activities (Allen & Currie, 2012).

Rituals provide students with a structure for connecting with the teacher and with one another (H. A. Davis et al., 2012).

The prefrontal cortex of the brain and its working or short-term memory is freed to do higher-level thinking when routines and procedures are used (Sprenger, 2008).

If students are to have equitable opportunities to act appropriately, behavioral expectations must be clearly stated (B. M. Davis, 2006).

If you want students to consider your classroom as their home, be sure that they know what the expectations are the minute they walk through the door (Allen, 2010).

Rules need to be written in the affirmative, be brief, and be posted in the classroom (Tileston, 2004).

Rituals that announce an arrival, departure, beginning of an activity, or celebration can instantly engage students (Jensen, 2005a).

The following steps apply when teaching and reviewing classroom procedures:

- Explain the activity before the activity actually happens.
- Role-play the procedure.
- Practice the procedure, and make certain that students understand.
- Provide feedback on the accuracy of the implementation.
- Reteach the procedure as needed.
- Review the procedure prior to implementation every time during the first few weeks of school.
- Review the procedures following holidays. (Burden, 2000)

HOW: CLASSROOM APPLICATION

- Examine every part of each period or of the entire school day, and determine what specific procedures students need to learn so that the classroom operates efficiently and effectively. For example, decide what students will do when they enter the room. Will there be a sponge activity on the board? Are students allowed to talk quietly? Once you have determined your procedures or rituals, have students role-play or practice them until they get them correct. Provide feedback after each practice, and celebrate when students perform the rituals to your satisfaction. A recommended list of celebrations is contained in Chapter 16.

- Save your voice for teaching, and use other things to assist you with management. If you do not have a way of getting students' attention, either you will spend your time yelling over their voices or you will spend an inordinate amount of time waiting for them to get quiet. Teachers have shared with me the following techniques as ways they have of getting students' attention when they need it without shouting:

  ○ I use the key of *G* from a xylophone that I strike with a mallet. Other teachers use chimes or hotel or door bells. If you Google *resonator bells,* you will find a xylophone where each of the colored keys of an octave has its own mallet and can be used separately by eight different teachers.

- o Teacher uses a rain stick and turns it upside down. By the time it stops *raining,* the class is quiet.
- o Teacher says, *"Class."* Students say, *"Yes."* Teacher varies the way he or she says, *"Class,"* and the class responds in the same way, such as, *"Class, class,"* and students say, *"Yes, yes."*
- o Teacher says, *"Red Robin."* The class says, *"Yummmm"* (as in the commercial to advertise Red Robin restaurants).
- o Teacher claps a pattern. Students clap back the same pattern.
- o Teacher stands on a carpet square in the front of the room. When the teacher is on the square, students know to quiet down and listen.

- One way to provide specific feedback on your rituals is to tell students, on a scale of 1 to 10, how they are performing. For example, when using chimes to get students' attention, have them role-play talking to a partner and then becoming quiet as soon as they hear the signal. When they get quiet upon hearing the chimes, let them know how well they did. If students rate a 5, then discuss what specific behaviors need to be practiced for students to move toward perfection, a 10. Continue to practice until they move in the appropriate direction. Celebrate when a 10 is earned!

- If you do a good job of teaching your expectations and procedures, you may need very few rules or even no rules at all. I have visited classrooms where there were so many rules that even the teacher could not keep up with them. Here are a few tips for making decisions regarding the rules you need in your classroom.

- o Limit your rules to three to five maximum.
- o Make sure each rule is stated briefly and in the affirmative, thereby telling students what to do instead of what not to do. For example, when a student is running down the hall, rather than saying, *"Don't run,"* a better request would be *"Please walk!"*
- o Rules should be visually posted as a constant reminder of your expectations.

- A student teacher in my class related that her college professor told her that she needed only two rules. They are as follows: *Be nice* and *be safe.* Your question may become this: *Then how do we handle students who come to school without the needed supplies?* Do what my daughter Jennifer did. For students who do not have a pencil, she has a jar on her desk filled with the ugliest pencils she can find. They are called *nubs.* Students do not want to write with *nubs,* and they never get stolen. In addition, collect ugly discarded copy paper for the students who come to class without paper. No students should be allowed to sit and do nothing simply because they come without tools.

• During the first few days of school, have students participate in determining the rituals and rules of your classroom. Students will be more likely to support procedures and rules that they helped create. Teachers have shared with me that the rules students generate are often stricter than the ones that the teacher intended.

• Teach students enough sign language so that you can communicate with them by signing your procedures. For example, when you need students to listen to what you are saying, make the sign for listen and have students sign back to you. When you need them to stop what they are doing, make that sign as well. What a pleasure to have students complying with your requests without saying a word!

• Use energetic music to set time limits on an activity that involves movement or talking. Select a song with a motivational rhythm, and play it softly as students complete a task, such as meeting an appointment or reviewing content with a close partner. By the time the song ends, students must have completed their conversations and be ready in case you call on them to respond.

• Use catchy phrases, chants, rhymes, or raps during transition times. Vanessa Anderson, a teacher at Cleveland Elementary School in Spartanburg, South Carolina, uses the following rap as her fifth- and sixth-grade boys transition from one subject area to another:

One, Two	What should we do?
Three, Four	Listen up once more.
Five, Six	My hands and legs are fixed.
Seven, Eight	I'm sitting up straight.
Nine, Ten	I'm ready for learning again.

By the time the class finishes reciting the rhyme, students have all the necessary materials out and available and are in their seats, ready for the next lesson. I observed this ritual working beautifully in her class.

• Rather than wait for students to forget or fail to comply with a procedure and then reprimand them, cue them about the expected behavior prior to the procedure. Cues are reminders of the appropriate behaviors prior to a particular task or event. Cues increase the likelihood that the proper behaviors will be followed and probably need to be used until the expectations and procedures become a habit in students' brains, which takes approximately 21 days or 28 times, whichever comes first.

• When students are having difficulty comprehending your expectations and procedures, a T-chart may be warranted. T-charts delineate exactly what behaviors are expected of students and can be beneficial for teaching social skills as well. For example, often teachers will have a rule that states *respect one another.* The problem is that different students have different definitions of the term *respect*. Design a T-chart around the word *respect*. Have students brainstorm ideas as to what respect looks like and sounds like (see the example below). Post the T-chart as a constant reminder of what the specific behaviors are that you expect whenever you ask a student to comply with the rule *respect one another*.

T-Chart

Respect

Looks Like	Sounds Like
One person talking at a time	"Please"
Taking turns	"Thank you"
Heads nodding in agreement or disagreement	"I disagree"
Smiles	"Excuse me"
Eye contact	"Your turn"
Undivided attention	Applause

REFLECTION

> **What are the specific rituals or procedures I need for effectively managing my classroom?**

_____

_____

_____

_____

_____

_____

_____

_____

_____

_____

_____

_____

_____

_____

_____

_____

_____

_____

_____

_____

15

Accentuate the Positive

The brain learns best when it is not in high stress.

Marcia L. Tate

WHAT: CREATING AN AFFIRMING CLASSROOM ENVIRONMENT

I am a trainer for *The 7 Habits of Highly Effective People.* During that workshop, a concept is taught called the *emotional bank account.* The *emotional bank account* is a metaphor for the relationships that we establish with one another. We make deposits (positive interactions) and withdrawals (negative interactions) in other people's emotional bank accounts. However, just as in the case of financial accounts, if you make larger or more frequent withdrawals than you make deposits, you are soon overdrawn or even bankrupt with that person.

Let's apply this concept to the classroom. Many teachers have overdrawn or bankrupt relationships with their students because they spend the majority of their time trying to think of all the consequences or punishments (withdrawals) that can be administered to stop unacceptable behavior. This puts the teacher and student on the negative side of their emotional bank accounts. Now, change the paradigm. Let's find more ways to positively affirm the good things that students do (deposits) so that, when we have to make a withdrawal, we have at least built up a positive account with the student. In fact, solid relationships are built when, for every withdrawal, there are 8 to 10 deposits. In other words, for every time in class I have to reprimand a student or give a consequence for misbehavior, there should be many more times that I have complimented the same student for good or improved behavior and acceptable class work. If you look for the good in students, you can find it!

The deposits many teachers use involve extrinsic rewards. There is evidence from the field of economics that they do have their place (Lazear, 2000). Football players have stickers on their helmets as indicators of exceptional performance. Stickers, stars, privileges, and so on appear to provide positive reinforcement for desired behaviors. In fact, extrinsic rewards tend to be more effective when they are tied to the student's specific performance and not to the student him- or herself.

The field of psychology, however, lends a word of caution to this scenario. Rewards can inhibit performance and appear to become negative reinforcers in the long term (Deci, Koestner, & Ryan, 1999). Affirmations, celebrations, choice, feedback, and peer interactions can be more effective for the increased long-term motivation of your students.

WHY: THEORETICAL FRAMEWORK

Positive discipline rewards desired behaviors and attempts to be nonpunitive by ignoring, rather than punishing, misbehavior (Pinto, 2013).

Good discipline should be supported with the following three positive goals: (1) *demonstrate*—model the positive behaviors that you desire from your students; (2) *facilitate*—expect all students to be successful; (3) *motivate*—use copious rewards such as a private smile or public praise to acknowledge a student's improved behavior (Allen & Currie, 2012).

Consider the following guidelines when using classroom rewards:

- Give frequently in the early stages of learning and less as the students internalize appropriate behaviors.
- Reward the behavior you want students to repeat, using the weakest reward required to strengthen the behavior.
- A reward that works for one student may not work for another.
- Be sure that every student is capable of being successful on the task.
- Minimize extrinsic rewards while maximizing intrinsic ones. (Silver, 2012)

As praise is only a verbal reward, and encouragement is an acknowledgment of a student's effort, encouragement is preferable (Pinto, 2013).

Praise can be powerfully motivating if given when a student accomplishes specific performance goals (Marzano, Pickering, & Pollock, 2001).

Giving a reward signals that the task itself is undesirable because, if the task were desirable, a reward would not be necessary. To get the same compliance, the reward will have to eventually increase (Pink, 2009).

Learned optimism and hope are crucial factors essential for making high achievers of low-socioeconomic-status students (Jensen, 2009).

The brain releases the chemical dopamine when people engage in activities that make them happy, providing them pleasure and increasing the likelihood that the behavior will be repeated (Sousa, 2009).

Effective teachers strive to catch students being good and make certain that their parents know about it as well (Orange, 2005).

Neuroscientists have found that the expectation of a reward has the potential to be just as addictive as alcohol or other drugs (Pink, 2009).

HOW: CLASSROOM APPLICATION

- Be certain that your classroom exudes a positive learning environment—one that is both physically and psychologically safe. A positive environment includes smiles, friendly greetings, student support for one another, celebrations—and the absence of sarcasm or threats, which shut the brain down to learning or higher-level thinking. Your room may be the one bright spot in a student's otherwise dismal day.

- Get acquainted with each student personally, and call them by name daily. That is much more difficult to do at the middle and high school levels when you have multiple classes; however, it is still essential to building a positive environment. Stand at the door each morning or period, and warmly greet students each day. Take a personal interest in students. If you know that one played on the football team during the weekend, ask him whether he won the game. If a student has a new hairdo, positively comment on the change. You would be surprised what a positive difference these simple comments can make to your relationship with a student!

- Teach your students to follow your rituals for effective classroom management. If you must have some rules, make sure they number no more than three to five. Be certain that they are stated positively so that they tell students what to do rather than what not to do.

- Use rewards such as stickers, stars, and coupons sparingly. Whenever they are used, be certain that they are tied to students' specific performance or effort and not to the students' intellect or ability.

- Some students who are consistently having trouble following your procedures may need individual behavior charts. The chart should list no more than one or two behaviors you will be observing for each individual student. Whenever you see the student exhibiting those behaviors, a check mark can be made on the chart. When the student has a designated number of daily checks, the student is entitled to some type of predetermined reward.

- Provide students with choice whenever possible as a positive alternative to rewards. For example, allow students to engage in a variety of instructional strategies when delivering content (see the list in the Engage the Brains of Your Students section in the Introduction), or give them several ways to demonstrate what they have learned on an assessment. Allow them to select who they will make appointments with to discuss class content. When students have choice, they feel some measure of control over their environment.

- Notify parents via telephone or email when their children have done something exceptional. This simple technique will have two results. You will be indirectly making a deposit in the student's bank account, while the parents will be so surprised at a positive contact from you that they will be simultaneously making a deposit to their child's account as well.

- Because the brain loves celebration, celebrate even minor, but deserved, successes in the classroom. Let students know that you appreciate their improved efforts by incorporating the 33 celebrations outlined in Chapter 16 of this book.

- Play music with motivating lyrics and an enthusiastic beat to create a positive environment. Examples of songs are included in Chapter 5.

- Provide students with specific reasons for praise. If you walk around the classroom consistently saying, "Very good! Great! Excellent! Great job!" day after day, students will be very tired of the rhetoric in a very short amount of time. However, if you find specific reasons to congratulate students for a job well done, the effect is much greater. For example, tell Julie that the opening paragraph of her paper used so many descriptive adjectives that it grabbed the reader's attention from the very beginning. Tell Marvin that you noticed he was able to stay in his seat for a longer period today and that you really appreciate the effort.

- There appear to be three major types of positive reinforcers: tangible reinforcers, privileges, and social reinforcers.

  - Tangible reinforcers include candy, stickers, treats, and other types of rewards given for specific positive behaviors displayed. This is the least desirable type of reinforcer, and its use often leads to the student asking this question: *If I complete this assignment, what do I get?*
  - Privileges include extra computer or recess time, being appointed line leader or student of the day, or being given a no-homework pass or a spot in the high school parking lot. These are better than tangibles as positive reinforcers but are still not the best.
  - The final type is the social reinforcer. These include verbal praise, hugs, handshakes and other forms of celebration, positive notes or phone calls home to parents, and written comments to the student. This is the preferred type to use because, in the real world, adults receive social reinforcers most often. For example, I don't think I have ever gotten a sticker for cooking a good dinner, but I have received a compliment from my husband or children for a delicious meal. If your students are always looking for tangibles or privileges, then at the very least, pair the tangible with a social reinforcer. In other words, tell the students why they are receiving the candy or no-homework passes. Then, gradually reduce the number of tangibles or privileges given, but keep the social reinforcers coming. They're good for the brain!

REFLECTION

> **What are 10 things I can do to create a positive learning environment in my classroom?**

_____

_____

_____

_____

_____

_____

_____

_____

_____

_____

_____

_____

_____

_____

_____

_____

_____

_____

_____

_____

_____

16

Celebrate Good Times, Come On!

I Just Want to Celebrate!

Rare Earth

WHAT: CELEBRATIONS AND THE BRAIN

At the end of the course *Worksheets Don't Grow Dendrites,* which I teach to administrators and teachers all over the world, we celebrate the vast amount of information that we have learned. Some participants say that they learn more from me in one day than they learn in some workshops in several days. We move eight steps to the left and right to the song "Celebration" by Kool and the Gang. This culminating activity practically ensures that participants will leave the workshop with a feeling of euphoria and jubilance.

The brain loves celebrations! If you don't believe that, then you haven't noticed what happens when a sports team achieves. When a baseball player hits a home run, players high-five that player all the way into the dugout. When a soccer player scores the winning goal, the entire team might run out on the field and lay out on top of the winning player. Sometimes, college football players are even charged with excessive celebration! No matter how small the improvement, students and their teacher should show their appreciation for increases in student learning or behavior by a preponderance of celebrations. This chapter will provide more than 30 ways that students and teachers can create a positive climate through celebrations and affirmations.

In more classrooms than I care to count, I have observed students who make a habit of pointing out the imperfections in the personalities, looks, and abilities of their classmates. They make sarcastic remarks, demean, and deride one another—sometimes to get attention, sometimes to feel more in control, and sometimes just to be mean.

In a brain-compatible classroom where threats are diminished and confidence increased, no place exists for this negative type of behavior. Threats place the brain in survival mode and make it difficult, if not nearly impossible, to learn at optimal levels. This is why, in Maslow's hierarchy, survival and psychological needs are placed below academic pursuits. Survival needs must be satisfied before academic needs are even taken into consideration.

When a teacher affirms a student's correct answer or when students celebrate the accomplishments of a peer, a cooperative group, or the class as a whole, confidence increases, and the classroom becomes a place where behavior problems are diminished and learning accelerated.

WHY: THEORETICAL FRAMEWORK

When students learn something new, the learning should be celebrated (Allen & Currie, 2012).

The talents and unique life experiences of students can be celebrated with the recognition of their birthdays and special accomplishments (H. A. Davis et al., 2012).

Celebrations cause students to laugh. Humor helps students to make a personal connection with the teacher (Chapman & King, 2003).

Celebrations provide students with feelings of pride, joy, and success (Allen & Currie, 2012).

Even small improvements in behavior along the way should be celebrated. It is not necessary to wait until students achieve extraordinary results (Patterson, Grenny, McMillan, & Switzler, 2008).

Be certain that an affirmation or celebration is deserved. Students must feel that their performance warrants the celebration (Jensen, 2003).

The more positive acknowledgments the student gets, the better; however, teachers should praise the student's specific accomplishments rather than the student him- or herself (Divinyi, 2003).

Positive feedback just may be the single most powerful influence on the brain's chemistry and an essential element in helping people develop a healthy self-concept (Sylwester, 1997).

HOW: CLASSROOM APPLICATION

- *Bell Ringer.* Purchase a small bell, and ring it only when students' answers show great insight or their performances demonstrate great creative effort.

- *Bravo! Bravo!* Have students stand, clap their hands, and shout, *"Bravo! Bravo!"* just as an audience would do following an outstanding concert or performance. This celebration should be reserved for exceptional performances.

- *Celebration Music.* Select exuberant songs that will motivate students and help them celebrate their successes, for example, "We Are the Champions" by Queen; "Celebration" by Kool and the Gang; "I Got the Power" by Snap; "Gonna Fly Now," the theme from *Rocky;* "New Attitude" by Patti LaBelle; "Shining Star" by Earth, Wind, and Fire; or "I Just Want to Celebrate" by Rare Earth.

- *Clam Clap.* Have students show a snapping motion with both hands to simulate a clam opening and closing.

- *Clappers.* Purchase plastic hand clappers from a novelty store. Whenever students give a correct answer or behave appropriately, give them a hand with the plastic clappers. They will feel so good about themselves! These clappers can also be purchased from the Oriental Trading Company catalog.

- *COOL!* The word *cool* is made with the fingers and eyes. Take your right hand and make the letter C with your thumb and forefinger. Place that C beside your right eye. Stretch your eyes wide to make the two Os in the word *COOL.* The L is made by turning the palm of the left hand toward you, making the letter L with your thumb and forefinger, and turning the other three fingers down. Place the letter L next to your left eye so that your fingers and eyes form the word *COOL.* Say the word *COOL* with expression as you form the word.

- *Fantastic! Fantastic!* Have students raise their hands, put them on either side of their faces, and fan their faces as they say, with expression, *"Fantastic! Fantastic!"*

- *Fantastic! Fantastic! (2.0).* Tell students that their performance is fantastic by pretending that you are pressing the spray on a bottle of Fantastic. Make the appropriate noises for a spray bottle as you are pretending to press the spray three times. Then, with the same hand, pretend you are wiping two times while you say, *"Fantastic! Fantastic!"* with expression. Students can also *spray* one another.

- *Finger Clap.* Have students take the forefingers of the left and right hands and gently clap them together. There should be no sound made at all.

- *Firecracker.* Have students place their hands together and move them into the air much as a firecracker would. They should also make the sounds of a firecracker going into the air. Then, they should clap their hands once, separate them, and bring them down slowly while making the sounds of a firecracker's sparks descending.

- *Golf Clap.* Have students pretend they are at a golf game. Have them gently pat their hands together as if applauding the performance of a golfer who has just made a hole in one. They must look prim and proper as they gently clap their hands together. Students can give one another golf claps.

- *Good Job, Good Buddy!* Have students pretend that they are drivers in 18-wheelers. Have them pretend that they are pulling the cord with their dominant hand, and make the sound a truck makes when it is blowing its horn. Then say, *"Good job, good buddy!"*

- *Good Job! Good Job!* Have students spell out *Good Job! Good Job!* by saying, *"G- double O- D- J- O- B. Good job! Good job!"* while clapping two times on the *Good job! Good job!*

- *Great! Great! Great!* To tell students that their performance is *great, great, great,* spread your dominant hand out to represent the grater. Your other hand forms a fist to become the ball of cheese. Then, pretend to be grating the cheese while you say, *"Great! Great! Great!"*

- *Handshake.* Extend your dominant hand, and shake the hand of a student when that student does something noteworthy. Students can give one another handshakes to show their appreciation for a job well done.

- *High Five.* The high five has always symbolized agreement or acceptance. To high-five, raise the open palm of your dominant hand and slap the raised open palm of the dominant hand of a student when that student does something well. Have students high-five their learning partners or other students in their cooperative group when the group successfully completes an assignment.

- *Kiss Your Brain!* Tell a student who has given a good answer to *"Kiss your brain."* The student should then take his or her dominant hand and place it on the lips and then on the top of the head.

- *Light of Intelligence.* Get a magic wand that lights up, and rename it to be either a *light of intelligence* or a *positive energy stick.* When a student does something noteworthy, shine the light on the student. I have one that I use in my workshops, and even adults love it. It lights up at the end and makes a sound when you push a button. To get one like mine, go to www.tool-trainers.com.

- *Light Up!* Buy a rubber lightbulb. You may purchase one from Spencer Kagan's catalog. When students are obviously thinking, show them that you appreciate their efforts by passing them the lightbulb to hold temporarily. Holding the lightbulb is indicative of the *light coming on* in the students' brains.

- *Looking Good!* Take the forefingers of both left and right hands, and make the four sides of an imaginary mirror. Make sure you make sounds as you are forming the sides. Then, once your mirror is made, if you are female, primp in it by turning your head to the right side and patting the back of it, while you say emphatically, *"Looking good! Looking good!"* If you are male, however, pretend to be combing your hair, while you say the words. If you have no hair, pretend that you are shining your bald head with a rag, so you move the imaginary rag back and forth, back and forth, while saying, *"Looking good! Looking good!"*

- *Marshmallow Clap.* Have students extend their hands out with the palms facing and pretend that they are going to clap. However, their hands never meet because there is a marshmallow in between the hands. This is the favorite celebration of several of my classes!

- *Microwave.* Have students take the little finger of the right hand and wave it without waving the rest of the hand, therefore, creating a little wave. By the way, if you go to Australia, do not have students do the *Microwave.* In Australia, that gesture means something unmentionable. If you are ever at one of my workshops, I will be happy to tell you in person what it means. However, I cannot tell you in this book.

- *Original Cheers.* When students are working in cooperative groups, or *families,* encourage them to create original cheers that do not last more than a few seconds. Groups can perform these cheers for the class and use them whenever a member of the family, or the family as a whole, does something exceptional. Often, the entire class's performance will be noteworthy. Then, all families can perform their cheers simultaneously.

- *Outstanding!* To tell a specific student that his or her performance is outstanding, have each student make a baseball umpire's signal for an *out* and then stand up. This cheer is reserved for the highest quality of answers.

- *Pat on the Back.* Have students take their dominant hand, reach across their bodies, and pat themselves on the back when they give a correct answer or behave appropriately.

- *Round of Applause.* Have students softly clap their hands together, but as they clap them, have them move their hands around in a large circle so that they literally have a *round of applause.*

- *Seal of Approval.* Have students extend their arms and turn their palms outward, clapping and making a noise like a seal.

- *Silent Cheer.* Have students hold up both left and right hands beside their head and cheer as enthusiastically as possible; however, no sound at all should come from the lips. This is the same sign made when the deaf cheer.

- *Spider Clap.* Have students spread their fingers apart on both hands and then clap the fingers on their right hand together with the corresponding finger on the left hand so that the fingers resemble a spider.

- *Standing O!* Have students give one another *standing Os* by standing on their tiptoes and forming an *O* with their arms raised above their heads while saying the letter *O* aloud. This cheer is reserved for truly exceptional answers or performances!

- *Thumbs-Up.* Give students a thumbs-up to indicate agreement or acknowledgment of a job well done. To form a thumbs-up, make a fist with your dominant hand while pointing the thumb of that hand toward the ceiling. Students can give thumbs-ups to one another when they agree with a peer's answer.

- *Who Did a Good Job? You!* Using the same expression as the chant *"Who Let the Dogs Out?,"* have students say with expression, *Who did a good job?"* And then, say, *"You,"* while pointing to the student whose performance excels.

- *WOW!* Make a *W* by sticking up only the three middle fingers of your right hand. Place those three fingers to the right side of your mouth. Then form your mouth into a large *O.* Finally, stick the three middle fingers of your left hand beside the left side of your mouth. Say the word *wow* with expression as you make the same word with your fingers and mouth. Students can give one another a *WOW* when the performance is deserved.

REFLECTION

> ### Which celebrations will I use in my classroom to affirm my students and commemorate successful performances?

_____

_____

_____

_____

_____

_____

_____

_____

_____

_____

_____

_____

_____

_____

_____

_____

_____

_____

17

Use Low-Profile Interventions

Teach on your feet, not in a seat!

Marcia L. Tate

WHAT: INTERVENING APPROPRIATELY

I was observing in a classroom a few years ago when I noticed the following scenario. A history teacher was lecturing from the front of the room when she noticed that a student was paying little attention to the lecture. Instead, the student appeared to be intently interested in a page in his history book. However, the teacher also noticed that there was something protruding from under the history book. Upon practicing proximity and moving closer to the student, the teacher observed a cell phone inserted in the history book from which the student was texting. Prior to this time, I was the only one who knew that this was going on, and I only knew because the student's desk was directly in front of where I was seated in the rear of the room.

The angry teacher felt compelled to point out the disciplinary infraction to the entire class. She indicated to the class how disgusted she was with the student and requested sarcastically that he read his text message aloud to the entire class. The student responded with a smart-aleck remark. Soon both teacher and student were involved in a shouting match that ended when the teacher ordered the student out of her classroom.

This entire incident could have been avoided if the teacher had used a *low-profile intervention.* Low-profile interventions are techniques that proactive teachers use that are likely to correct misbehavior without negatively impacting the teacher's ability to deliver instruction. A low-profile intervention, in the above scenario, would have been to move closer to the student and tap the desk lightly, indicating to the student that the cell phone should be put away—all the while continuing to teach. In this way, the behavioral infraction may have been resolved without the entire class being aware of what was happening and having to endure the disruptive effects of a power struggle. Other low-profile interventions include the following: eye contact, signaling, pausing, ignoring, proximity, and touching.

WHY: THEORETICAL FRAMEWORK

Teachers' use of verbal and nonverbal behaviors predicts how credible students think those teachers are, how motivated students are, and how willing they are to comply with teachers' requests (Burroughs, 2007).

Private signals and attempts to redirect the behavior of students are considered forms of *gentle discipline* (Reeve, 2006).

Eye contact from the teacher seems to quiet students down immediately because, when students are making eye contact with the teacher, they find it difficult to talk at the same time (Smith, 2004).

"Telling students that a request is a *Nike Issue* means that they should *Just Do It* without arguing or negotiating, even if they don't want to do it" (Divinyi, 2003, p. 77).

Teachers should speak in a clear, direct, and firm yet soft voice when addressing the class (Smith, 2004).

Signaling, reminding, warning, praising, and ignoring are all forms of *low-key discipline* (Kottler, 2002).

The following nonverbal and nonpunitive responses may be used to get students back on task:

- ignoring
- nonverbal signals
- proximity or standing near a student
- supportive touching (Burden, 2000).

Proximity, or moving near students while teaching, helps to keep their attention focused (Smith, 2004).

The following low-profile interventions can be effective in redirecting students back to the task:

- Use the student's name in a lesson.
- Use humor, not sarcasm, directed at the situation or yourself.
- Send an *I-message* to remind students that their behavior affects other students.
- Use positive phrasing by stating the way in which appropriate behavior can lead to positive outcomes.
- Remind students of the rules.
- Provide students with choices. (Burden, 2000).

HOW: CLASSROOM APPLICATION

- Some teachers are masters of the low-profile intervention of eye contact. Simply looking at students without saying a word can be very effective, especially if they know that you mean business. My father was a minister and a master of eye contact. If my sisters and I were talking while he was preaching, he would give us *the look.* We would not want to go home if we had gotten *the look.* We would ask members of the congregation if we could go home with them!

"Are you trying to maintain class control with eye contact, or are your contact lenses bothering you?"

• Reminding students of the specific procedures that are required (cueing) prior to the implementation of an activity helps to ensure that students comply with established rituals. See Chapter 14 for additional information regarding the process of cueing.

• When certain forms of misbehavior become apparent, move closer to the offending student in the hope that your proximity will eradicate the infraction. For example, if two students are talking at the back of the room while you are teaching at the front, practice proximity, and move closer to the students without making mention of their conversation. Keep teaching!

• A hand on a student's shoulder can be a low-profile intervention that provides a calming touch to a misbehaving student. Make sure the touch is truly calming and not antagonistic.

- Incorporating the student's name in an example may refocus his or her attention. Be sure that the name is not used in a derogatory way. For example, I was teaching special education students to take a word problem and set it up as an algebraic equation. Instead of starting with the problems in the book, I made up a real-life problem using the names of three students in the room regarding a visit they may have made to the movies. All the students were intently interested in solving this actual problem where they bought tickets, popcorn, drinks, and candy.

- Use *I-messages* when addressing misbehavior, such as "I was disappointed when you failed to show up for class on time" or "I can never allow students in this class to ridicule one another because we are a family and work together." Putting the emphasis on you rather than the student de-escalates the situation.

- When you use a ritual to get students' attention, such as ringing chimes or raising your hand, and students do not get quiet immediately, simply pause until you get what you want. If you talk over their talking you send the message that what you have to say to students is not nearly as important as what students have to say to one another.

- When students are becoming upset and raise their voices when talking to you or a classmate, most teachers have a tendency to raise their voices as well. Do the opposite. When students raise their voices, lower yours. It will calm, rather than escalate, the situation. Remember, *Shouting Won't Grow Dendrites.*

- If rules or procedures are posted on your wall, simply pointing to a rule without speaking can remind students that they may not be complying with it.

- Find a teacher who knows sign language, and get him or her to teach you enough signs to manage your students. I have been in classrooms where teachers only use their voices to teach but not to manage. They sign directions to the students such as *Sit down, stop, and listen* or courteous words such as *please, thank you, you're welcome.* The students then sign back to the teacher. When done correctly, it works extremely well and makes the classroom a calming place to be.

REFLECTION

> **What are some low-profile**
> *interventions* **that I can use to correct misbehavior**
> **while continuing to teach?**

_____

_____

_____

_____

_____

_____

_____

_____

_____

_____

_____

_____

_____

_____

_____

_____

_____

_____

_____

_____

_____

18

De-emphasize the Negative

While laughter may heal you, high stress may kill you.

Marcia L. Tate

WHAT: CONSEQUENCES FOR MISBEHAVIOR

When I teach my *Worksheets Don't Grow Dendrites* course, I engage participants in an unforgettable activity in which they pair up and become Partners A and B. Partner A asks Partner B to extend his or her dominant arm out to the side and not allow it to be pushed down. Partner A asks Partner B to simultaneously think of something positive in his or her life or something that makes him or her feel good or smile. While the arm is extended, Partner A pushes down on the shoulder, while Partner B tries not to allow the arm to be pushed down. The arm typically stays strong and cannot be pushed down no matter the pressure. Partner A then asks Partner B to think of a time when he or she was extremely upset, angry, or stressed and repeats the procedure. The arm invariably goes down, and everyone is amazed. The procedure is then repeated with the roles reversed.

If people cannot keep their arm strong when under threat, how are students going to learn to read or learn calculus when under threat? They can't! This is the reason that Maslow's hierarchy of needs places survival needs below the ones leading to academic success. Those have to be taken care of first so that the brain can be freed to think at higher levels!

The purpose of this activity is to convince people of the body's reaction when the brain is thinking both positively and negatively. For example, when the brain is thinking positively, the arm stays raised due to the body's ability to appropriately perform when the brain has confidence and is thinking good thoughts. This is the reason that a baseball player will often get a hit and then come back later in the game and get another hit. After all, success breeds success! When the brain is thinking negatively, the arm is pushed down easily due to the fact that anger, stress, and fear are all threats to the brain. When the brain is threatened, it prepares the body to defend itself against the threat by shifting blood to the survival part of the brain and to the extremities. Because blood flow is reduced in the frontal lobe, one is not able to think at higher levels, and the body does not perform appropriately. This is why a baseball player who makes one error will often make another one. This is also the reason that a stressed or angry teacher is not capable of making the best decisions regarding effective consequences for students. When both teacher and student are affected, power struggles ensue, and no one truly wins. Even if the teacher orders the student out of the room, the student has received the attention or power that he or she desired all along.

There appear to be three reasons that teachers continue using ineffective discipline methods: (1) behaviors are deeply embedded when they are learned through imitation and observation; (2) habits are difficult to break; and (3) when ineffective methods work part of the time, teachers believe that, if they are persistent, the methods will work again (Koenig, 2000).

Proactive classroom managers create a positive classroom environment in which confidence is encouraged and threat discouraged, where students feel both physically and psychologically safe. They know that, while consequences may stop misbehavior in the short term, it is the positive interactions that change behavior in the long run. When disruptions do occur, these teachers first try a low-profile intervention, as described in the previous chapter. If they have to resort to a high-profile intervention or implement a consequence, they do so in a calm manner, demonstrating the respect for the

"Obedience school was okay, but the teacher responded to my unwanted behavior with penalties. I never learned any long-term behavior modification, so I'm still barking and ignoring orders."

student that they also expect for themselves. They send the message to the student that they care about him or her but will not tolerate the inappropriate behavior that the student has chosen.

A consequence is defined as something that a student would not want to happen but is not physically or psychologically harmful to the student. Consequences are more effective than punishment because, in the real world, there are both positive and negative consequences for the decisions that people make, and people are usually aware of those consequences prior to making a decision. This chapter will list some possible consequences that may work. I mean *may* because each student is different. What works for one may or may not work for another. In fact, many students have experienced such severe consequences, either at home (such as verbal or physical abuse) or at school (such as suspension or expulsion), that one more consequence in a long list will probably make little difference.

While this chapter will examine what the research says about consequences for misbehavior, keep in mind that there are teachers who are so skilled that they do not use consequences at all. Instead, they spend their time equipping students with the skills necessary to exhibit the appropriate behavior in all circumstances.

WHY: THEORETICAL FRAMEWORK

Cortisol, a hormone released when the brain is under severe threat, can prevent the brain from forming a new memory or accessing memories already formed (Allen & Currie, 2012).

Because teenagers rely more on the emotional part of the brain, called the amygdala, and not the rational frontal lobe, they have difficulty anticipating the consequences of their behavior (Feinstein, 2009).

Decades of research show that zero tolerance approaches have a questionable effect on student achievement and can ignite student hostility and resentment (Brown, 2009).

The U.S. achievement gap is directly proportional to the punishment gap. African American students are six times more likely to be suspended than to receive a diploma that enables them to enter college (Yang, 2009).

Four enemies of learning that cause the brain to shut down are threat, high stress, anxiety, and induced learner helplessness (Jensen, 2007).

Angry proactive teachers note their anger and calmly state what the student needs to do. Reactive teachers choose to take their anger out on students (Orange, 2005).

Threats not only diminish memory, but they also decrease creativity and higher-order thinking skills (Jensen, 2007).

(Continued)

(Continued)

"The old model of *my way or the highway* is ineffective for today's students and results in a major waste of human life and resources" (Tileston, 2004, p. 2).

Natural or logical consequences, those attached to student behavior, enable students to see the connections between the choices they make and the consequences (Smith, 2004).

Complaining in the teacher's lounge about how terrible your students are may win you sympathy temporarily but is counterproductive and only reinforces the false assumption that students are purposely setting out to make your life miserable (Kottler, 2002).

HOW: CLASSROOM APPLICATION

- Proactive classroom managers believe in their ability to maintain a well-run classroom and assist students in their ability to manage themselves. Therefore, they are not overheard making any of the following comments: *This is the worst class I have ever had! I don't know what to do with Don! What can you expect when you're teaching these kids?* A well-managed classroom begins with the teacher's belief and visualization that the year will be a great one.

- Be certain that students are fully apprised of your classroom management plan with its rituals or rules, celebrations or rewards, and consequences. Give students a written copy of your plan for students to share with their parents. You may want to have parents sign the plan to ensure that they have reviewed it. Role-play the behaviors you want from students, and practice the rituals and provide feedback until students' performance is satisfactory. Once students know your expectations, then it is their choice to comply or not. Having students assist in formulating your management plan for the class helps them take more ownership of it.

- When dealing with an angry student, if the student raises his or her voice, lower yours. You have the power to escalate or de-escalate any volatile situation in your classroom.

- Conduct a private conference with the student to address the misbehavior. Oftentimes, students who misbehave don't know any alternative behaviors that would be more acceptable than the ones that got them in trouble in the first place. For example, if a student is used to hearing profanity in the home, then that behavior is acceptable. Explain why it is not acceptable at school, and recommend what should be said or done in lieu of the unacceptable language.

- When talking with the student, calmly use *I-messages,* which put more of the emphasis on you and not the student. An example of an

I-message is as follows: I was disappointed when you chose to disrupt the class. *I-messages* are not as effective when students are extremely angry.

- The most appropriate negative consequences proceed naturally from the misbehavior. For example, a student who purposely knocks over his or her milk should be asked to clean it up, or a student who makes a mean comment to another should apologize for the insult.

- Deprive the student of a classroom privilege (such as free time or a desirable activity). Prior to the disciplinary infraction, be certain the student knows that loss of a privilege is a possible consequence, so you can make it clear that to engage in the misbehavior is a choice the student has made.

- Ask a student who is misbehaving to remove him- or herself from the other students, and place him or her in a location in the room known as *time-out*. The student goes to time-out without work or anything else to do; however, provide the student with an opportunity to rejoin the rest of the class when he or she is willing to be cooperative. When asking the student to move to the time-out area, simply state the request politely. If the student does not move, request again. If that does not work, do not force the student to go. Simply say, *"I understand that you do not choose to go to time-out. We will discuss this later."* Then continue teaching.

- If misbehavior persists, contact parents, and inform them of the disciplinary infraction. Be sure to convey that you have the best interest of their child at heart and are desirous of working with them to ensure academic achievement. Work with the parents to formulate a plan for the discontinuance of the misbehavior. It is crucially important that, the first time you contact a parent, the interaction should be a positive one. Either prior to school starting or as soon as possible after the school year begins, contact the parent by phone or in writing, and tell him or her how pleased you are to be working with his or her child. Tell him or her that you are expecting to have a great year and are primarily concerned with the success of the child. If the first contact is positive, the parent will be more supportive if contacted for a negative reason.

- While writing should never be used as punishment, having older students create written reflections regarding their misbehavior appears to work in some cases. Students in the intermediate grades or in middle or high school can be required to engage in a reflective writing activity in which they describe the circumstances surrounding the occurrence of the misbehavior, state exactly what the misbehavior was, and state what specific behaviors they can engage in that would lead to a better outcome in the future. The following three questions can be answered:

  ○ What happened?
  ○ How did you respond?
  ○ How will you respond differently next time?

- Students could be removed from the classroom and sent to in-school suspension, a designated room in the school where students are held for a number of hours or days. Students should be provided with academic work and not allowed to talk with other students. Lunch is brought to the student, who works in a confined space. Be certain that being in in-school suspension is undesirable. If it becomes a place where students can be removed from a class that they didn't like in the first place and allowed to socialize with their friends, then it is more of a reward than a consequence.

- Students who persist in misbehavior can be excluded from the class and sent to another room. To employ this consequence, simply arrange ahead of time to pair with a fellow teacher at a very different grade level. You take their students, and they take yours. Students are sent for a designated period of time with academic work. The students in the receiving class are told ahead of time to ignore the arriving student. The misbehaving students are told they have chosen not to comply with the rules of this class and are therefore being sent to another room. This consequence should be used very sparingly but can be very effective as a fifth grader, for example, would not want to be seen in a third-grade classroom.

REFLECTION

> ### What consequences will be effective in my classroom? (Remember that consequences may be necessary, but their use should be limited because they tend not to change misbehavior for most students.)

_____

_____

_____

_____

_____

_____

_____

_____

_____

_____

_____

_____

_____

_____

_____

_____

_____

_____

DETOUR

Deal Proactively With Challenging Behavior

19

Get Help With Chronic Behavior Challenges

Students who have constant behavior problems often have very negative feelings about learning, school, and even about themselves.

Sousa, 2009

WHAT: MANAGING THE DIFFICULT TO MANAGE

My son, Chris, loved school when he was in the lower grades. He made As and Bs on his report card each semester. In the fourth or fifth grade, his love for school began to diminish. This continued through middle school and into high school. Eventually, his grades also diminished proportionately. At first, we thought the decline was due to a lack of motivation and that he just wasn't trying. Therefore, we decided to withhold privileges from him until he improved his grades. However, that just did not happen! Everything had been taken away from him other than the air he breathed, and we observed no change in his academic performance. Chris was not a major behavior problem, but he was having difficulty staying in his seat and concentrating on the task at hand.

In desperation, we had a more in-depth diagnosis made, and the doctor surmised that Chris was exhibiting all of the characteristics of ADD. The doctor suggested that he could have a shortage of dopamine in the frontal lobe of the brain. Dopamine is a chemical that assists the brain in focusing and attending to tasks. When you consider that one way the brain produces dopamine is through the body's movement, is it any wonder that ADD students move around, even when they're not supposed to?

As Chris's classes did not afford him the opportunity to experience the very thing his brain needed most, movement, we placed him in a different school where he could be involved in active engagement strategies—project-based instruction, service learning, drawing, the use of manipulatives, field trips called knowledge treks, and so on. Chris's report card in the first reporting period at his new school yielded five As and one B. We had not seen As and Bs since the primary grades.

You have to understand that, while my son experienced challenges in school, he, like other students (especially males), has several gifts. He draws beautifully, can assemble anything with his hands (without looking at the directions), and is a whiz on the computer. There are plenty of job opportunities for Christopher. However, unless teachers use the 20 instructional strategies delineated in the introduction of this book, Chris and other students like him will not experience success in school.

Chris is not alone. I cannot count the many parents I have spoken with whose children exhibit some of the same characteristics as my son. ADD is but one of the chronic challenges that teachers have to deal with. This chapter will describe six of a teacher's major behavior challenges and make some research-based generalizations for meeting the needs of these students.

It is important to note that, while this chapter delineates several symptoms of each chronic disorder, few students exhibit characteristics of just one. In fact, the term *comorbidity* (overlapping conditions) is used to describe the fact that your greatest behavior challenges reflect symptoms from several different disorders, making it difficult to discern exactly which disorder takes precedence. Therefore, the majority of classroom application activities in this chapter will apply regardless of the specific disorder. Eric Jensen's (2011) text *Different Brains, Different Learners: How to Reach the Hard to Reach* (2nd ed.) is an exceptional resource for a more in-depth description of the six chronic behavior challenges summarized below and additional disorders as well.

Attention Deficit Disorder and Attention Deficit Hyperactivity Disorder

Children are designed to be active. It is when that activity supercedes the majority of their peers and when children may have difficulty focusing that the behavior becomes a disorder called ADHD. ADD is probably the most frequently diagnosed chronic behavior disorder of students. While the number of American students diagnosed with ADD has increased more than seven times since 1990, nearly 80 percent of those students taking medication for the disorder are male ("Pay Closer Attention," 2004). The brain of the ADD child experiences difficulty distinguishing environmental (external) from mental (internal) states, moving from other directed to self-directed, distinguishing the here and now from the future, and delaying immediate gratification (Jensen, 2000b). In other words, students with ADD tend to be impulsive and have a difficult time taking care of their day-to-day responsibilities that require appropriate timing. More

"How come the History Channel is so interesting and my history class is so boring?"

than 33 percent of students with ADD appear to have as many as four or more behavioral or cognitive issues. These include stress disorder, depression, oppositional disorder, learning disorder, and conduct disorder.

ADHD must be diagnosed by a licensed professional, but likely causes may include genetic transmission (70 to 95 percent of all cases of ADHD are genetically transmitted); brain differences such as reduced size and activity in the frontal lobe and basal ganglia due to decreased amounts of the neurotransmitter dopamine; exposure to environmental toxins; insufficient parental nurturing coupled with fast-paced and violent images on television shows; or poor nutrition, including excess sugar and processed foods with additives and preservatives.

Symptoms of ADD include, but are not limited to, the following:

- poor concentration and short-term memory
- messy or poorly organized desk or area
- becoming frequently distracted
- constantly moving or fidgeting
- inability to plan sufficiently for future happenings, being unprepared
- poor time management
- impatient and unable to delay gratification
- acting before thinking
- inability to learn from past mistakes and apply to future decisions
- shouting out answers in class or inability to complete schoolwork

Conduct Disorder

Often called the predecessor to psychopathic behavior, conduct disorder is probably a teacher's greatest challenge. It is an antisocial, pathological, and extremely disruptive pattern of behavior. Unlike oppositional defiant disorder (ODD), conduct disorder is highly tied to violent behavior. It is also more prevalent with male than female students and has both environmental and genetic components. Males with lower levels of the stress hormone cortisol can show symptoms of conduct disorder because they seem to be unafraid of consequences (Jensen, 2011). Some people hypothesize that increases in violence and stressors, poor nutrition, overcrowded schools, a more sedentary lifestyle, and increased *in-your-face talk* can lead to more incidences of conduct disorder (Jensen, 2011).

Symptoms of conduct disorder include, but are not limited to, the following:

- lack of acceptable social skills
- no guilt or regard for how others feel
- impulsivity without regard for consequences
- willfully bullying or hurting others
- being consistently disrespectful and cruel to teachers and classmates
- using profanity and other forms of verbal abuse
- committing random acts of violence and destruction against animals and people
- refusing to follow stated directions
- blaming others for one's own shortcomings
- perceiving classmates as hostile or threatening

Learned Helplessness

Learned helplessness, a very serious and chronic condition, occurs when students believe that a certain outcome is inevitable whether or not they respond to the situation. They are often seen as withdrawn and passive because they perceive a lack of ability to control what happens to them. In other words, students with learned helplessness believe that, regardless of what they do, they will not be successful, so why even try. Due to the lack of content relevancy and hands-on learning in the upper grades, learned helplessness is more prevalent in junior and senior high school students than elementary ones. It can also be found in students of low socioeconomic status, males, and epileptics and can often accompany signs of depression.

While serious, learned helplessness is considered a condition, not a disorder, and therefore the learned behaviors can be unlearned. Likely causes include neglect, particularly during the first few years; a perceived lack of control during a traumatic life event; teachers or parents who do too much for students and keep them from experiencing their own failures; or teachers or parents who label students as lazy or stupid, causing the students to attribute their failures to character flaws.

Symptoms of learned helplessness include, but are not limited to, the following:

- decreased amounts of dopamine, serotonin, and epinephrine in the prefrontal cortex of the brain
- believing that one has no control over one's environment
- making statements like *Who cares? So what? Why even try?*
- listlessness and inactivity
- remaining passive even when events are shocking
- lack of hostility, even when needed
- increased sarcasm
- lack of motivation
- cognitive problems
- loss of appetite and weight

Oppositional Defiant Disorder

ODD, caused by a combination of both genetic and environmental factors, is a chronic disorder of one's personality. Students who exhibit this disorder tend to be aggressive, aggravating, and confrontational and possess a seemingly utter disregard for how other people feel. Unlike students with conduct disorder, these students are not typically violent, although they can be very deceitful, hostile, and aggressive. The ODD child's opposition to all authority figures is constant and pervasive. The number of students with the symptoms of oppositional disorder appears to have increased over the last generation and usually shows up by age 8. When paired with ADD, oppositional disorder represents the most common psychiatric concern in children.

According to Eric Jensen (2000a), as society devalues respect and politeness, the number of students with oppositional disorder is likely to increase. Other likely causes are an inherent personality that is more demanding and rigid; exposure to sexual or physical abuse, neglect, divorce, or head trauma; parents who are addicted to alcohol; or a serotonin system in the brain that is dysfunctional.

Symptoms of ODD include, but are not limited to, the following:

- arguing with adults and peers
- refusing to follow adult direction, requests, or rules
- becoming angry and resentful
- intentionally annoying others
- becoming easily annoyed by others
- cursing or using inappropriate language
- possessing low self-esteem
- losing one's temper very easily
- blaming other people for the mistakes one makes
- becoming vindictive without cause

Acute Stress Disorder and Depression

Chronic stress is one of the three major sources of the lack of motivation in middle and high school students. The other two are use of marijuana and learned helplessness, which were discussed earlier in this chapter. Stress is the body's way of responding physiologically to a perceived lack of control over an aversive situation. About 18 to 20 percent of children in America have acute or chronic stress disorders. These students will experience some of the characteristics of posttraumatic stress disorder and may even experience a marked decrease in the number of cells in the brain stem. When a student's brain is in a high state of stress, it secretes large amounts of cortisol and may respond in one of two ways: either by becoming numb or desensitized to the stress around it or by becoming hypervigilant or always on alert for the next threatening occurrence. Likely causes include a traumatic life event, especially in the early years of a child's life; prenatal distress; unsafe schools; a high resting heart rate above 94 beats per minute; a dysfunction in the frontal area of the brain that regulates scheduling and prioritizing; or the disruptions and chaos often associated with low-income families (Jensen, 2011).

Symptoms of acute stress disorder include, but are not limited to, the following:

- increased irritability and aggressiveness
- numbing of responsiveness or decreased energy
- recurring recollections of the traumatic event
- hypervigilence or increased startle response
- difficulty sleeping
- loss of interest in things once enjoyed
- reduced affection
- lack of ability to concentrate on the task at hand
- increased rote or automatic behavior
- increased use of drugs such as marijuana and cocaine

Depression, a chronic, pervasive mood disorder, affects both the mind and body of a student. In fact, it is now believed that teens experience depression much more than was once thought. According to the American Academy of Pediatrics, more than half a million children are taking medication for depression. After puberty, the percentage of female students experiencing some form of depression soars (Jensen, 2000a). Within the last 40 years, suicide rates have tripled.

There are several different types of depression: major depression, the most common type; dysthymia, a less-serious type typically lasting for several years; bipolar depression, which results in extreme highs and lows in one's personality; seasonal affective disorder, which follows the rhythm of the seasons of the year; and posttraumatic stress disorder, which can be triggered by natural disasters, life-threatening illnesses, physical abuse, or the sudden death of a loved one (Jensen, 2011). Most episodes of depression last approximately 9 to 12 months and, with treatment, improve within a year.

Some of the more common causes of depression include brain irregularities such as an imbalance in neurotransmitter levels, a dysfunction of inflammatory mediators called cytokines or a hippocampus that is 5 to 12 percent smaller than normal; chronic or acute stress; children who are sheltered from life's challenges; reduced amounts of sunlight; smokers who attempt to quit; vitamin and mineral deficiencies; and a dysfunctional style of parenting.

Symptoms of depression include, but are not limited to, the following:

- lack of interest in most activities
- persistent sadness, anxiety, or apathy
- trouble concentrating
- decreased energy or increased fatigue
- irritability or uneasiness
- decreased or increased appetite resulting in weight change
- inability to sleep at night or too much sleep
- aches and pains that cannot be explained
- recurring thoughts of death or suicide
- fluctuation between extreme highs (reckless behavior, impulsivity, and great schemes) and extreme lows (withdrawal, apathy, and sadness)

WHY: THEORETICAL FRAMEWORK

ADD affects up to 10 percent of the population, three times as many boys as girls, and is characterized by impulsiveness, inattention, and often hyperactivity (Sylwester, 2010).

In 2003, ADHD became the most diagnosed school-age disorder in the United States (Jensen, 2011).

Considering that the frontal lobe of many ADD students is underdeveloped, it is unrealistic to expect them to perform identically on assessments as students who have not been identified as having ADD (Willis, 2006).

An increased level of testosterone resulting in an enlarged amygdala in the male brain is believed responsible for greater aggressiveness and at-risk behavior by boys (Feinstein, 2009).

Learned helplessness is not genetic but an adaptive response to the circumstances of life when students feel unrelentingly hopeless (Jensen, 2009).

When students have experienced traumatic classroom experiences, those experiences can trigger states of learned helplessness due to feelings of anxiety or resignation regarding the content (Jensen, 2007).

Students with a sense of learned helplessness have the flawed perception of themselves that they lack the skills or abilities necessary to complete the assigned tasks (Reyes, 2011).

(Continued)

(Continued)

When children are raised in an abusive environment, they learn that, in order to get their needs met, they too need to be violent or aggressive (Jensen, 2011).

Chronic and acute stress levels can be significantly increased by exposure to violence in the family (Emery & Laumann-Billings, 1998).

ODD accounts for a minimum of half of all referrals to mental health professionals and is more common in boys before puberty and almost equal in boys and girls after puberty (Jensen, 2011).

Approximately 28 percent of American youth will have experienced an episode of major depression by the age of 19 (Lewisohn, Rhode, & Seely, 1998).

Because the prefrontal cortex of the brain is not mature, events that adults would consider inconsequential appear huge to teens and can cause them undue stress (Willis, 2006).

Exposure to chronic stress actually shrinks memory cells in the frontal lobe of the brain, which is responsible for planning, making judgments, and regulating one's ability to be impulsive (Cook & Wellman, 2004).

HOW: CLASSROOM APPLICATION

• Play calming music as students enter your classroom, during transition times, or when students are engaged in creative tasks. Classical, jazz, Celtic, Native American, or new age music enables the brain and body to relax and places the brain in more of a state conducive for learning. Set up a listening station or use earphones when you desire that only certain students avail themselves of specific music. See Chapter 5 for additional information on the use of music in the classroom.

• Make your classroom highly predictable by establishing your routines and procedures from the first day of school and practicing them until they become habitual. Open and close class the same way daily. Make transitions predictable. Your ADD student, especially, will thank you. When there does need to be a change in the routine, make students aware of the change prior to its implementation.

• The 20 brain-compatible strategies delineated in the introduction of this book are not only necessary for the 90 to 95 percent of the students whose behavior can be controlled by using the activities in the first 18 chapters; they are also essential for the 5 to 10 percent whose chronic behavior disorders make your life and the lives of your students challenging, to say the least. When students have the opportunity to visualize themselves being successful and growing in confidence, when they are actively engaged in strategies that require bodily movements such as role playing, drawing, project-based instruction, work study, or field trips, and when your classroom becomes one in which students see humor, not sarcasm, then and only then can you come closer to producing students who leave your classroom significantly improved academically, emotionally, and physically. Perhaps if these strategies were used with all students from the first day of school, many chronic behavior problems would never surface.

- Intervene early with students who display symptoms of these chronic behaviors. Early intervention appears to correlate with a reduction in antisocial behavior as the student ages. For example, with a conduct-disordered student, the most appropriate time to make a change in the behavior is prior to kindergarten or at least by first grade. By the time this student has become a juvenile, it is much more difficult and often too late (Jensen, 2000a).

- Maintain a positive learning environment in which students can develop a sense of confidence that comes from building on their personal strengths. Celebrate even minimal progress or success that moves the behavior in the intended direction. Catch all students doing something right, and praise them for it. Keep progress charts and implement point systems that enable students to earn privileges or affirmations.

- For the ADD or ADHD student, focus on the following: reinforce positive behaviors and rechannel negative ones, avoid threats and distress, provide external reinforcers such as points or extra recognitions, establish routines, use more movement, communicate with students in writing, and teach them how to manage time (Jensen, 2011).

- The following recommendations are made for dealing with the child with ADD:

  o Provide images for students to look at when not paying attention to what the remainder of the class is doing.
  o Involve students in short-term memory activities during the morning hours when they are more focused.
  o Teach using a variety of the multiple intelligences to honor the strengths of all students (see Table 9.1 in Chapter 9).
  o Determine class rituals and rules, and stick to them.
  o Positively reinforce students for appropriate behaviors.
  o Provide opportunities for students to move.
  o Introduce new material in multisensory ways. (Sprenger, 2002)

- Remain strong but calm. Any anxiety or overt anger on the part of the teacher who is dealing with these chronic behavior challenges either is a sign of weakness or serves to escalate the confrontation and make the behavior worse. An attitude of calm and strength sends the message that, while you are in support of the individual student, you will not tolerate the inappropriate behaviors in your classroom, and you cannot be persuaded or threatened to think otherwise.

- Always separate the chronic behavior from the student, realizing that the behavior represents what they are doing and not who they are personally. Examine the situation to ascertain the reason behind the symptoms displayed in class and what you can do to positively affect the disorder, not just temporarily treat the symptoms.

- For students who exhibit symptoms of conduct disorder, focus on the following: provide a positive environment, don't believe their stories without proof, make specific requests, be consistent, give privileges rather than rewards, and share your plan with the student (Jensen, 2011).

- For students who exhibit symptoms of learned helplessness, focus on the following: engage their brain in positive states, be energetic and enthusiastic, maintain a good relationship, and challenge them through enriching experiences (Jensen, 2011).

- Students who experience learned helplessness feel a lack of control over what they are experiencing. A sense of control can be encouraged through the following: providing students with choices and discussing the consequences of those choices, supplying students with an overview of the day's activities in advance, allowing them time to journal and discuss with others, and incorporating movement into the lesson (Sprenger, 2002).

- For children who exhibit symptoms of ODD, focus on the following: agree on rewards and consequences in a behavioral support plan, respond in a nonconfrontational way, confirm stories before you believe them, and remain consistent (Jensen, 2011).

- For students who exhibit symptoms of stress disorder or depression, focus on the following: be personal and positive, and take time to connect with them; use more movement; establish structure and routines; teach stress-reduction techniques such as deep breathing, yoga, singing, visualization, and movement; and encourage goal setting (Jensen, 2011).

- Do not attempt to deal with any of the aforementioned disorders by yourself. You were probably not trained specifically in this area and must insist on the support of a team of people within and outside the school. This team should consist of any of the following persons: the student's parents or guardians, an administrator, a school counselor, a social worker, a psychiatrist, and the student. Do not perceive this request for support as a sign of weakness. True strength lies in knowing when assistance is warranted so that your classroom can remain the best possible learning environment for every student. For example, my daughter Jennifer, who taught second grade, dealt with a student whose mother was cocaine addicted when he was born. As a result, he exhibited some characteristics of conduct disorder and learned helplessness. The student carried on conversations with several different personalities and was my daughter's biggest challenge that school year. However, with the help of the student's psychiatrist, whom he sees several times a week, progress was made. The psychiatrist's records were shared with a team who developed an individual plan of support for the student.

- With the support team described above, sit down and make a definitive plan for what will happen with a student when he or she demonstrates certain chronic behaviors. Make sure that each member of the team has input into the plan and that consensus is reached on what the plan will include. In this way, manipulative students cannot play one member of the team against another, and the student will realize that the adults in his or her life are forming a united front. The plan should include the answers to some of the following questions:

  - What strengths does this student have that can be recognized and built upon?
  - What kind of skills need to be developed in this student, and how can we specifically go about developing those skills?
  - What is the time frame for the development of the necessary skills?
  - Where should this student sit in the room?
  - Which of the classroom rules will be enforced and which overlooked in the case of this student?
  - What will be the plan if this student disrupts class, bothers another student, or refuses to do the assigned work?
  - What will be the plan if this student becomes violent or throws a temper tantrum?
  - When is the best time for the support team to meet, and how often? (Jensen, 2000a)

- Break the content and the accompanying activities into chunks so that even students with short attention spans remain focused. Tell students how much time they have for each learning segment, and provide warnings prior to the time to change to the next activity.

- With oppositional, conduct disordered, or other strong-willed students, smile and request a change in behavior. Then, move away from the student's space. For example, if John is talking out of turn, simply say, "John, would you consider not talking when I am talking?" and then move away from the student's desk.

- Work study is one of the most prevalent brain-compatible strategies used in alternative schools throughout the country. These schools are populated by middle and high school students who, for whatever reason, have been suspended or expelled from traditional school. Many of these students are there because they have demonstrated symptoms of the chronic behavior challenges that we have been discussing. Work study, which includes apprenticeships, internships, and other forms of on-the-job training, not only provides students with active engagement but supplies them with the life purposes that are so sorely lacking. When students in alternative schools can spend time reading once or twice a week to the senior citizens in a retirement home; design original pieces of artwork to be sold to the community; plant flowers to beautify the school campus; or plan, cook, and serve delicious meals to the culinary delight of all who partake, positive brain chemicals are produced, and negative self-perceptions are replaced with confidence. A confident student seldom disrupts. In my house hangs a beautiful painting that represents the creative efforts of a student in McArthur South Alternative School in Miami, Florida, where I taught for several days. Every time I look at that painting, I have hope.

• Maintain a close, positive relationship with the parents or guardians of a child with chronic behavior disorders. In the case of students with conduct or oppositional disorder, one cannot assume that the students are telling the truth as they often play one person against another. By keeping in close contact, the truth can be corroborated.

• Consult Chapter 15: Accentuate the Positive and Chapter 18: De-emphasize the Negative for additional classroom activities that may work with your most challenging students as well as all others in your room.

REFLECTION

> ## What is my plan for dealing with the chronic behavior disorders in my classroom?

Attention Deficit Disorder and Attention Deficit Hyperactivity Disorder (ADD and ADHD)

_____

_____

_____

Conduct Disorder

_____

_____

_____

Learned Helplessness

_____

_____

_____

Oppositional Defiant Disorder (ODD)

_____

_____

_____

Stress Disorder and Depression

_____

_____

_____

Other Chronic Disorder

_____

_____

_____

20

Solicit
Parental Support

Parents are their children's first and best teachers.

Marcia L. Tate

WHAT: PARENTS ON YOUR SIDE

Just because this is the last chapter in the book does not mean it is any less important than the 19 chapters that precede it. Just as I don't believe that any teacher gets up in the morning with the intention of not doing a good job at teaching, I also don't feel that any parent gets up in the morning determined to be the worst possible parent he or she can be. In most cases, I surmise that parents are doing the best they can based on their knowledge, skills, experiences, and the circumstances in which they find themselves.

While the job of a parent is so important, it also does not come with a manual. There are very few courses, if any, to prepare parents for the mammoth job that they are about to undertake. If there were an ad placed for the job of a parent, if might read like Figure 20.1.

If this ad truly did appear in your local paper, would you hurry to apply? Who would?

As an educator and a parent of three, I know that both jobs are arduous assignments. Many teachers and administrators view today's parents with emotions that range from cautious optimism to downright disdain. There is a reason for the variations in feelings toward parent support and involvement. According to McEwan (2002), many parents of students today tend to be more personally informed and actively engaged in education but also less respectful of authority and more cynical, distrustful, stressed, angry, and worried than ever before. On the other hand, some parents appear not to care at all.

McEwan (2002) further states that parents are displaying increased hostility for some of the following reasons: a failure of the school to communicate, educators' unwillingness to keep commitments, educators becoming defensive when practices are called into question or being

Figure 20.1

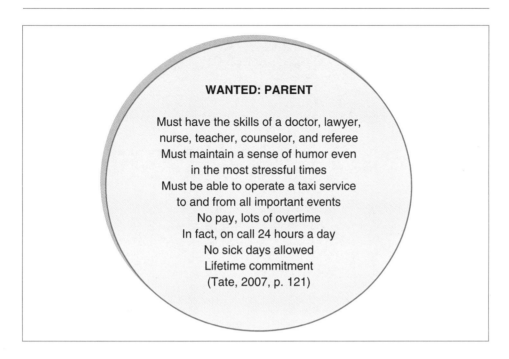

WANTED: PARENT

Must have the skills of a doctor, lawyer,
nurse, teacher, counselor, and referee
Must maintain a sense of humor even
in the most stressful times
Must be able to operate a taxi service
to and from all important events
No pay, lots of overtime
In fact, on call 24 hours a day
No sick days allowed
Lifetime commitment
(Tate, 2007, p. 121)

unable to apologize when an apology is warranted, or educators being unwilling to give parents credit for truly understanding their children and having insight into school challenges.

In Chapter 15, we discussed the concept of the emotional bank account. Let's apply that to the teacher–parent connection. Let's suppose that the first contact a parent has with you at the beginning of the school year is negative. For example, school has just started, and you call to complain because Johnny is out of his seat when he's not supposed to be. Well, you are on the deficit side of Johnny's parents' bank account, and the year has just begun. If these negative contacts (or withdrawals) continue, then soon you are overdrawn with this parent and may even bankrupt the relationship. When parents stop taking your calls and refuse to attend parent–teacher conferences, you might want to consider that you are involved in a bankrupt relationship.

It is so vitally important that the initial contact with a student's parent be positive. This contact can determine whether you establish a yearlong supportive or adversarial relationship with the most important people in your students' lives. This positive phone call, or deposit, helps to ensure that, if it becomes necessary for you to make a withdrawal (a contact for a negative reason), there will be a balance in the account.

Whether dealing with two-parent families, single-parent families, teen parent families, stepparent families, or no-parent families, students excel when their teacher and parent or caregiver enjoy a positive relationship (Rudney, 2005). Just as in proactive classroom management, proactive, positive relationships with parents can result in fewer reactive interactions and angry confrontations.

"Angry parents on lines 1, 2, 3, 4, and 5."

WHY: THEORETICAL FRAMEWORK

Noticing how each student's family impacts the student's physical and emotional health is critical to a successful classroom (Cooper & Garner, 2012).

School leaders need to be sure that parents and teachers can create a unified vision of family engagement practices (Glasgow & Whitney, 2009).

The chronic stress that parents in poverty experience negatively affects their ability to parent, and negative or disengaged parenting impairs children's performance in school (Jensen, 2009).

In order to know who they are teaching, teachers need to be familiar with local businesses, places of worship, and issues impacting the community (Cooper & Garner, 2012).

To build strong, long-lasting relationships with parents, schools should identify critical areas of need and offer that content in on-site programs for parents (Jensen, 2009).

When parents and teachers are partners in educating students, a more unified home–school effort exists, and they are less likely to lay blame on one another when anything is amiss (Orange, 2005).

Parents who give teachers the most difficulty can be described as follows:

- the parent who expects every teacher to cater to his or her individual needs

- the parent who is full of hostility and anger
- the parent who will never believe that his or her child can ever be responsible for any misbehavior
- the parent who manipulates the situation and works from a secret agenda
- the parent who is out of control
- the parent who has no earthly idea how to be a parent or to deal with the child's inappropriate behavior (Glasgow & Whitney, 2009)

When parents are involved in the schooling of their children, that involvement not only affects achievement but also influences what career choices and educational goals the child sets (Hill et al., 2004).

HOW: CLASSROOM APPLICATION

- Administrators should be encouraged to involve parents, business leaders, community members, and other stakeholders in strategic planning activities. Create surveys to solicit input on crucial school-related issues, and involve volunteers on teams that are trained to develop action plans to accomplish school goals and objectives. Parents will not object to plans they personally helped to develop.

- Administrators should determine who the key communicators are in the community. These are the movers and shakers who carry a great deal of influence and should be invited to the school and constantly kept abreast of the specific school goals and progress toward those goals.

- Prior to the beginning of the school year, if possible, make personal contact with every prospective parent. Call, write, or e-mail each parent, expressing your anticipation at having his or her child in your classroom for the year and informing him or her of your positive expectations for the child's success. If the initial contact is positive (a deposit), subsequent contacts will be more well received. This is much more easily accomplished at the elementary level. However, teachers at the middle and high school level could make the initial contact in writing or by e-mail.

- Secure the e-mail address of every parent willing to give it to you. Set up a file and a consistent system for informing parents of general information regarding your classroom, such as rituals and procedures, current academic objectives, upcoming field trips, assemblies, and so on.

- Create a Web page of your own, or become a part of your school's website. Post important class happenings, and communicate with parents as they access your site. Weekly homework assignments and dates for weekly, midterm, and final exams should be posted.

- Share your specific classroom management plan in writing with all of your students' parents. Have each student take a copy of the plan home, and have parents or guardians sign, stating that they have read the plan and discussed it with the student. For non-English-speaking parents, have the plan translated into the predominant language spoken by the students in your room.

- Take time to share the good news from your classroom in a newsletter or just a brief e-mail. Let parents know when students have great weeks following your rituals and procedures, when the average percentage of students passing your tests improves, or when an individual student excels. Shout the good news from the rooftops!

- Invite your students' parents or guardians to serve as volunteers in your classroom whenever possible. Once they see firsthand the awesome responsibility that you have as their child's teacher, they may be more supportive of what you are trying to accomplish. If you are not comfortable with them volunteering for you, recommend that they volunteer in another capacity in the school.

- Invite your students' parents or guardians to accompany the class on field trips and other class excursions. For example, my daughter Jennifer taught second grade. Each year, I would accompany her and her class to the holiday performance of the Atlanta Ballet's *Nutcracker*. Prior to the performance, the students and their parents dined with us at The Spaghetti Factory, a local restaurant. Not only did the excursion teach the students proper skills for formal dining, but they experienced the artistry of a beautiful ballet. There was also a side benefit that I don't believe my daughter even expected—the gratitude, support, and commitment of those parents who accompanied us. That support lasted for the remainder of the school year and beyond. My daughter was one of the most-loved teachers in her school by the parents of her students. She is now an instructional coach who works with multiple teachers and does not have her own class.

- When conducting a parent–teacher conference, be sure you adhere to the following guidelines:
  - Begin and end the conference on time.
  - Greet the parents cordially, and tell them how happy you are to have their child in your class and that you are looking forward to working together.
  - Share the purpose and agenda of the conference, and stick to it.
  - Share some positive news regarding the student's attributes or abilities.
  - If there is a concern, state the concern, and ask the parents what they think should be done about it.
  - Attempt to reach consensus as to next steps.
  - End with courtesy and a positive statement about future meetings.

REFLECTION

> What are some specific steps I can take
> to establish positive relationships with my
> students' parents or guardians?

_____

_____

_____

_____

_____

_____

_____

_____

_____

_____

_____

_____

_____

_____

_____

_____

_____

_____

Bibliography

Allen, R. (2008). *Green light classrooms: Teaching techniques that accelerate learning.* Victoria, Australia: Hawker Brownlow.

Allen, R. H. (2010). *High-impact teaching strategies for the "XYZ" era of education.* Boston, MA: Pearson Education.

Allen, R., & Currie, J. (2012). *U-turn teaching: Strategies to accelerate learning and transform middle school achievement.* Thousand Oaks, CA: Corwin.

Allen, R., & Wood, W. W. (2013). *The rock'n'roll classroom: Using music to manage mood, energy, and learning.* Thousand Oaks, CA: Corwin.

Armstrong, T. (2009). *Multiple intelligences in the classroom* (3rd ed.). Alexandria, VA: Association for Supervision and Curriculum Development.

Bender, W. N. (2008). *Differentiating instruction for students with learning disabilities: Best teaching practices for general and special educators* (2nd ed.). Thousand Oaks, CA: Corwin and Council for Exceptional Children.

Bender, W. N. (2012). *RTI in middle and high schools.* Bloomington, IN: Solution Tree.

Blaydes Madigan, J. (1999). *Thinking on your feet.* Murphy, TX: Action Based Learning.

Brown, J. F. (2009). Developmental due process: Waging a constitutional campaign to align school discipline with developmental knowledge. *Temple Law Review, 82,* 929–996.

Burden, P. R. (2000). *Powerful classroom management strategies: Motivating students to learn.* Thousand Oaks, CA: Corwin.

Burgess, R. (2000). *Laughing lessons: 149 2/3 ways to make teaching and learning fun.* Minneapolis, MN: Free Spirit.

Burke, K. (1992). *What to do with the kid who: Developing cooperation, self-discipline, and responsibility in the classroom.* Thousand Oaks, CA: Corwin.

Burroughs, N. F. (2007). A reinvestigation of the relationship of teacher nonverbal immediacy and student compliance-resistance with learning. *Communication Education, 56,* 453–475.

Canter, L., & Canter, M. (1993). *Succeeding with difficult students.* Santa Monica, CA: Canter.

Chapman, C., & King, R. (2003). *Differentiated instructional strategies for reading in the content areas.* Thousand Oaks, CA: Corwin.

Colbert, D. (2009). *Eat this and live! How to make simple food choices.* Lake Mary, FL: Siloam.

College Board. (2012). *Education professionals.* Retrieved from http://www.college board.org/prof

Cook, S. C., & Wellman, C. L. (2004). Chronic stress alters dendritic morphology in rat medial prefrontal cortex. *Neurobiology, 60*(2), 236–248.

Cooper, N., & Garner, B. K. (2012). *Developing a learning classroom: Moving beyond management through relationships, relevance, and rigor.* Thousand Oaks, CA: Corwin.

Costa, A. L. (2008). *School as a home for the mind: Creating mindful curriculum, instruction, and dialogue* (2nd ed.). Victoria, Australia: Hawker Brownlow.

Costa-Giomi, E. (1998, April). *The McGill Piano Project: Effects of three years of piano instruction on children's cognitive abilities, academic achievement, and self-esteem.* Paper presented at the meeting of the Music Educators National Conference, Phoenix, AZ.

Covino, J. K. (2002). Mind matters. *District Administrator, 38*(2), 25–27.

Crawford, G. B. (2004). *Managing the adolescent classroom: Lessons from outstanding teachers.* Thousand Oaks, CA: Corwin.

Davis, B. M. (2006). *How to teach students who don't look like you: Culturally relevant teaching strategies.* Thousand Oaks, CA: Corwin.

Davis, H. A., Gableman, M., & Wingfield, R. (2011). "She let us be smart": Low-income African American first grade students' understandings of teacher closeness and influence. *Journal of Classroom Interaction, 46*, 4–16.

Davis, H. A., Summers, J. J., & Miller, L. M. (2012). *An interpersonal approach to classroom management: Strategies for improving student engagement.* Thousand Oaks, CA: Corwin and Division 15 (Educational Psychology) of the APA.

Dean, G., Hubbell, E., Pilter, H., & Stone, B. (2012). *Classroom instruction that works: Research-based strategies for increasing student achievement* (2nd ed.). Alexandria, VA: Association for Supervision and Curriculum Development.

Deci, E. L., Koestner, R., & Ryan, R. M. (1999). *A meta-analytic review of experiments examining the effects of extrinsic rewards on intrinsic motivation.* Retrieved from http://www.selfdeterminationtheory.org/SDT/documents/1999_DeciKoestnerRyan_Meta.pdf

Dennison, G. E. (1990). *The big mission book.* Ventura, CA: Edu-Kinesthetics.

Dewey, J. (1934). *Art as experience.* New York, NY: Minion Ballet.

Dhong, H. J., Chung, S. K., & Doty, R. L. (1999). Estrogen protects against 3-methylindole-induced olfactory loss. *Brain Research, 824*, 312–315.

Dibble, S. (2008, January 22). District 203 provided spark for book: Psychiatrist draws connection between physical activity and learning. *Daily Herald* (Illinois) Retrieved from http://prev.dailyherald.com/story/?id=118011

Divinyi, J. (2003). *Discipline that works: 5 simple steps.* Peachtree City, GA: Wellness Connection.

Ekwall, E. E., & Shanker, J. L. (1988). *Diagnosis and remediation of the disabled reader* (3rd ed.). Boston, MA: Allyn and Bacon.

Emery, R. E., & Laumann-Billings, L. (1998). An overview of the nature, causes, and consequences of abusive family relationships: Toward differentiating maltreatment and violence. *American Psychologist, 53*, 121–135.

Erlauer, L. (2003). *The brain-compatible classroom: Using what we know about learning to improve teaching.* Alexandria, VA: Association for Supervision and Curriculum Development.

Feinstein, S. G. (2004). *Secrets of the teenage brain: Research-based strategies for reaching and teaching today's adolescents* Thousand Oaks, CA: Corwin.

Feinstein, S. G. (2009). *Secrets of the teenage brain: Research-based strategies for reaching and teaching today's adolescents* (2nd ed.). Thousand Oaks, CA: Corwin.

Fogarty, R. (2009). *Brain-compatible classrooms* (3rd ed.). Victoria, Australia: Hawker Brownlow.

Frasca-Beaulieu, K. (1999). Interior design for ambulatory care facilities: How to reduce stress and anxiety in patients and families. *Journal or Ambulatory Care Management, 22*(1), 67–73.

Gardner, H. (1979). The child is father to the metaphor. *Psychology Today, 12*(10), 81–91.

Gardner, H. (1983). *Frames of mind. The theory of multiple intelligences.* New York, NY: Basic Books.

Gardner, H. (1999). *Intelligence reframed: Multiple intelligences for the 21st century.* New York, NY: BasicBooks.

Gettinger, M., & Kohler, K. M. (2006). Process-outcome approaches to classroom management and effective teaching. In C. Evertson, C. M. Weinstein, & C. S. Weinstein (Eds.), *Handbook of classroom management: Research, practice, and contemporary issues* (pp. 73–95). Mahwah, NJ: Lawrence Erlbaum.

Glasgow, N. A., & Whitney, P. J. (2009). *What successful schools do to involve families: 55 partnership strategies.* Thousand Oaks, CA: Corwin and National Association of Secondary School Principals.

Glasser, W. (1999). *Choice theory: A new psychology of personal freedom.* New York, NY: HarperCollins.

Hammer, S. E. (1996). The effects of guided imagery through music on state and trait anxiety. *Journal of Music Therapy, 33*(1), 47–70.

Harmon, D. B. (1951). *The coordinated classroom* (Research paper). Grand Rapids, MI: American Seating Company.

Harris, J. R. (2006). *No two alike: Human nature & human individuality.* New York, NY: W. H. Norton.

Hattie, J. (2009). *Visible learning: A synthesis of over 800 meta-analyses relating to achievement.* New York, NY: Routledge.

Haycock, K. (2001). Closing the achievement gap. *Educational Leadership, 58*(6), 6–11.

Herz, R. S., Eliassen, J., Beland, S., & Souza, T. (2004). Neuroimaging evidence for the emotional potency of odor-evoked memory. *Neuropsychologia, 42*(3), 371–378.

Heschong, L. (1999). *Daylighting in schools: An investigation into the relationship between daylighting and human performance.* A study performed on behalf of the California Board for Energy Efficiency for the Third Party program administered by Pacific Gas and Electric as part of the PG & E contract 460–000.

Heschong Mahone Group. (2012). *Daylighting and productivity—CEC PIER.* Retrieved from http://www.h-m-g.com/projects/ daylighting/projects-PIER.htm

Hill, N. E., Castellino, D. R., Lansford, J. E., Nowlin, P., Dodge, K. A., Bates, J. E., & Pettit, G. S. (2004). Parent academic involvement as related to school behavior, achievement, and aspirations: Demographic variations across adolescence. *Child Development, 75*(5), 1491–1509.

Jabari, J. (2013). *Expecting excellence in urban schools: 7 steps to an engaging classroom practice.* Thousand Oaks, CA: Corwin.

Jensen, E. (1995). *Brain-based learning and teaching.* Thousand Oaks, CA: Corwin.

Jensen, E. (1998). *Sizzle and substance: Presenting with the brain in mind.* Thousand Oaks, CA: Corwin.

Jensen, E. (2000a). *Different learners, different brains: How to reach the hard to reach.* Thousand Oaks, CA: Corwin.

Jensen, E. (2000b). Moving with the brain in mind. *Educational Leadership, 58*(3), 34–37.

Jensen, E. (2001). *Arts with the brain in mind.* Alexandria, VA: Association for Supervision and Curriculum Development.

Jensen, E. (2003). *Tools for engagement: Managing emotional states for learner success.* Thousand Oaks, CA: Corwin.

Jensen, E. (2005a). *Teaching with the brain in mind* (2nd ed.). Alexandria, VA: Association for Supervision and Curriculum Development.

Jensen, E. (2005b). *Top tunes for teaching: 977 song titles and practical tools for choosing the right music every time.* Thousand Oaks, CA: Corwin.

Jensen, E. (2007). *Brain-compatible strategies* (2nd ed.). Victoria, Australia: Hawker Brownlow Education.

Jensen, E. (2008). *Brain-based learning: The new paradigm of teaching* (2nd ed.). Thousand Oaks, CA: Corwin.

Jensen, E. (2009). *Teaching with poverty in mind: What being poor does to kids' brains and what schools can do about it.* Alexandria, VA: Association for Supervision and Curriculum Development.

Jensen, E. (2011). *Different brains, different learners: How to reach the hard to reach* (2nd ed.). Thousand Oaks, CA: Corwin.

Jensen, E., & Dabney, M. (2000). *Learning smarter: The new science of teaching.* Thousand Oaks, CA: Corwin.

Jones, F. (2000). *Tools for teaching.* Santa Cruz, CA: Jones.

Joseph, R. (1999). Environmental influences on neural plasticity, the limbic system, emotional development and attachment: A review. *Child Psychiatry and Human Development, 29*(3), 189–208.

Kerman, S. (1979). Teacher expectations and student achievement. *Phi Delta Kappan, 60,* 716–718.

Koenig, L. (2000). *Smart discipline for the classroom: Respect and cooperation restored* (3rd ed.). Thousand Oaks, CA: Corwin.

Kottler, J. A. (2002). *Students who drive you crazy: Succeeding with resistant, unmotivated, and otherwise difficult young people.* Thousand Oaks, CA: Corwin.

Lazear, E. P. (2000). Performance pay and productivity. *American Economic Review, 90*(51), 1346–1361.

Lengel, T., & Kuczala, M. (2010). *The kinesthetic classroom: Teaching and learning through movement.* Thousand Oaks, CA: Corwin and Regional Training Center.

Levine, J., Baukol, P., & Pavlidis, I. (1999). The energy expended in chewing gum. *New England Journal of Medicine, 341,* 2100.

Lewisohn, P. M., Rhode, P., & Seely, J. R. (1998). Treatment of adolescent depression: Frequency of services and impact on functioning in young adulthood. *Depression and Anxiety, 7,* 47–52.

London, W. (1988). Brain/mind bulletin collections. *New Sense Bulletin, 13,* 7c.

MacLaughlin, J. A., Anderson, R. R., & Holic, M. F. (1982). Spectral character of sunlight modulates photosynthesis of previtamin D3 and its photo-isomers in human skin. *Science, 216*(4549), 1000–1003.

Madigan, J. B., & Hess, C. (2006). *Action based lab manual.* Murphy, TX: Action Based Learning Lab.

Markowitz, K., & Jensen, E. (2007). *The great memory book.* Victoria, Australia: Hawker Brownlow Education.

Marzano, R. J. (2007). *The art and science of teaching.* Alexandria, VA: Association for Supervision and Curriculum Development.

Marzano, R. J., & Pickering, D. J. (2011). *The highly engaged classroom.* Bloomington, IN: Marzano Research Laboratory.

Marzano, R. J., Pickering, D. J., & Pollock, J. E. (2001). *Classroom instruction that works: Research-based strategies for increasing student achievement.* Alexandria, VA: Association for Supervision and Curriculum Development.

McEwan, E. K. (2002). *10 traits of highly effective teachers: How to hire, coach, and mentor successful teachers.* Thousand Oaks, CA: Corwin.

Medina, J. (2008). *Brain rules.* Seattle, WA: Pear Press.

Michalon, M., Eskes, G., & Mate-Kole, C. (1997). Effects of light therapy on neuropsychological function and mood in seasonal affective disorder. *Journal of Psychiatry & Neuroscience, 22*(1), 19–28.

Muller, C., Katz, S., & Dance, L. (1999, September). Investing in teaching and learning: Dynamics of the teacher–student relationship from each actor's perspective. *Urban Education, 34,* 292–337.

National Reading Panel. (2000). *Report of the National Reading Panel: Teaching children to read: An evidence-based assessment of the scientific research literature on reading and its implications for reading instruction.* Washington, DC: National Institute of Child Health and Development.

Nevills, P. (2011). *Build the brain for reading—Grades 4–12.* Thousand Oaks, CA: Corwin.

O'Connor, P. D., Sofo, F., Kendall, L., & Olsen, G. (1990). Reading disabilities and the effects of colored filters. *Journal of Learning Disabilities, 23,* 597–603.

Orange, C. (2005). *Smart strategies for avoiding classroom mistakes.* Thousand Oaks, CA: Corwin.

Patterson, K., Grenny, J., McMillan, R., & Switzler, A. (2008). *Influencer: The power to change anything.* New York, NY: McGraw-Hill.

Pauli, P., Bourne, L. E., Diekmann, H., & Birbaumer, N. (1999). Cross-modality priming between odors and odor-congruent words. *American Journal of Psychology, 112,* 175–186.

Pay closer attention: Boys are struggling academically. (2004, December 2). *USA Today,* p. 12A.

Payne, R. K. (2001). *A framework for understanding poverty* (Rev. ed.). Highlands, TX: Aha! Process.

Pink, D. (2009). *Drive: The surprising truth about what motivates us.* New York, NY: Penguin.

Pinto, L. E. (2013). *From discipline to culturally responsive engagement: 45 classroom management strategies.* Thousand Oaks, CA: Corwin.

Read, M., Sugawara, A., & Brandt, J. (1999). Impact of space and color in the physical environment on preschool children's cooperative behavior. *Environmental and Behavior, 31*(3), 413–414.

Reeve, J. (2006). Teachers as facilitators: What autonomy-supportive teachers do and why their students benefit. *Elementary School Journal, 106*(30), 225–236.

Reyes, C. (2011). *When children fail in school part two: Teaching strategies for learned helpless students.* Retrieved from http://www.edarticle.com

Rickelman, R. J., & Henk, W. A. (1990). Colored overlays and tinted lens filters. *The Reading Teacher, 44*(2), 166.

Rosenthal, R., & Jacobson, L. (1992). *Pygmalion in the classroom: Teacher expectation and pupils' intellectual development.* New York, NY: Irvington.

Rudney, G. L. (2005). *Every teacher's guide to working with parents.* Thousand Oaks, CA: Corwin.

Ryan, R. M., & Deci, E. L. (2000). Self-determination theory and the facilitation of intrinsic motivation, social development, and well-being. *American Psychologist, 55,* 68–78.

Sapolsky, R. M. (2004). *Why zebra's don't get ulcers* (3rd ed.). New York, NY: Henry Holt.

Schnaubelt, K. (1999). *Medical aromatherapy: Healing with essential oil therapy.* Rochester, VT: Healing Arts.

Shaie, K. W., & Heiss, R. (1964). *Color and personality.* Bern, Switzerland: Hans Huber.

Silver, D. (2012). *Fall down 7 times get up 8: Teaching kids to succeed.* Thousand Oaks, CA: Corwin.

Smith, R. (2004). *Conscious classroom management: Unlocking the secrets of great teaching.* San Rafael, CA: Conscious Teaching.

Society for Developmental Education. (1995). *Pyramid of learning.* Peterborough, NH: Author.

Sousa, D. A. (2006). *How the brain learns* (3rd ed.). Thousand Oaks: CA: Corwin.

Sousa, D. A. (2009). *How the brain influences behavior: Management strategies for every classroom.* Thousand Oaks, CA: Corwin.

Sousa, D., & Tomlinson, C. (2011). *How neuroscience supports the learner-friendly classroom.* Bloomington, IN: Solution Tree.

Sprenger, M. (2002). *Becoming a wiz at brain-based teaching: How to make every year a best year.* Thousand Oaks, CA: Corwin.

Sprenger, M. (2003). *Differentiation through learning styles and memory.* Thousand Oaks, CA: Corwin.

Sprenger, M. (2005). *How to teach so students remember.* Alexandria, VA: Association for Supervision and Curriculum Development.

Sprenger, M. (2008). *The developing brain: Birth to age eight.* Thousand Oaks, CA: Corwin.

Sprenger, M. (2010). *Brain-based teaching in the digital age.* Alexandria, VA: Association for Supervision and Curriculum Development.

Sternberg, R. J., & Grigorenko, E. L. (2000). *Teaching for successful intelligence: To increase student learning and achievement.* Arlington Heights, IL: Skylight.

Sylwester, R. (1997). The neurobiology of self-esteem and aggression. *Educational Leadership, 54,* 75–79.

Sylwester, R. (2010). *A child's brain: The need for nurture.* Thousand Oaks, CA: Corwin.

Tate, M. L. (2005). *Reading and language arts worksheets don't grow dendrites: 20 literacy strategies that engage the brain.* Thousand Oaks: CA: Corwin.

Tate, M. L. (2007). *Shouting won't grow dendrites: 20 techniques for managing a brain-compatible classroom.* Thousand Oaks, CA: Corwin.

Tate, M. L. (2009). *Mathematics worksheets don't grow dendrites: 20 numeracy strategies that engage the brain.* Thousand Oaks, CA: Corwin.

Tate, M. L. (2010). *Worksheets don't grow dendrites: 20 instructional strategies that engage the brain* (2nd ed.). Thousand Oaks, CA: Corwin.

Tate, M. L. (2011). *Preparing children for success in school and life: 20 ways to increase your child's brain power.* Thousand Oaks, CA: Corwin.

Tate, M. L. (2012). *Social studies worksheets don't grow dendrites: 20 instructional strategies that engage the brain.* Thousand Oaks: CA: Corwin.

Thayer, R. (1996). *The origin of everyday moods.* New York, NY: Oxford University Press.

Tileston, D. W. (2004). *What every teacher should know about classroom management and discipline.* Thousand Oaks, CA: Corwin.

van Toller, S. (1988). Odors and the brain. In S. van Toller & G. Dodd (Eds.), *Perfumery: The psychology and biology of fragrance* (pp. 121–146). London, UK: Chapman & Hall.

Wallace, D. S., West, S. W., Ware, A., & Dansereau, D. F. (1998). The effect of knowledge maps that incorporate gestalt principles on learning. *Journal of Experimental Education, 67*(1), 5–16.

Willis, J. (2006). *Research-based strategies to ignite student learning.* Alexandria, VA: Association for Supervision and Curriculum Development.

Willis, J. (2007). *Brain-friendly strategies for the inclusion classroom.* Alexandria, VA: Association for Supervision and Curriculum Development.

Wong, H. K., & Wong, R. T. (1998). *The first days of school: How to be an effective teacher.* Mountain View, CA: Harry K. Wong.

Yazzie-Mintz, E. (2007). *Voices of students on engagement: A report on the 2006 high school survey of student engagement.* Bloomington: Indiana University, Center for Evaluation and Education Policy.

Yang, K. W. (2009). Discipline or punish? Some suggestions for school policy and teacher practice. *Language Arts, 87*(1), 49–52.

Index

Italicized page numbers indicate a figure.

Medina, J., 19, 53, 64
Memory
  ADD students and, 133
  amygdala, odor-evoked memory
    and, 53
  aromas and, 52, 53
  brain threats and, 71
  color and, 48, 49
  cortisol and, 119
  emotion and, 71
  episodic memory, 58, 60
  frontal lobe, chronic stress and, 132
  frontal lobe, willpower, limbic system
    and, 53, 119
  handwriting *vs.* typing and, 66
  long-term memory, 77
  muscle memory, 81–82
  music and, 41–42, 43
  procedural memory, 57, 81–82
  Proust effect and, 53
  semantic memory, 48
  short-term memory and, 95
  threats and, 71, 119
Metaphor strategy, 65, 67 (table)
Michalon, M., 38
Migraine headaches, 37
Miller, L. M., 19, 25, 94
Mind map, 50
Misbehavior
  achievement gap, punishment
    gap relationship and, 119
  appropriate negative consequences
    and, 121
  attention getting and, 30, 31
  boredom cause of, 11, 30, 31
  causes of, 29–31
  consequences for, 117–119
  expectations and, 26–27
  I-messages use and, 115, 120–121
  labeling and, 26–27
  lighting to prevent, 37
  movement as prevention of, 83, 85
  negative de-emphasis and, 117–119
  novelty and relevance as
    prevention of, 72
  positive affirmations and, 26–27, 101
  positive discipline and, 101
  power or control motivator of, 30
  private student conference and, 120
  privilege denial and, 121
  proactive *vs.* reactive teachers and, 119
  talking and, 75
  teacher proximity and, 114
  written reflections of, 121
  zero tolerance policy and, 119
  See also Chronic behavior challenges;
    Chronic behavioral conditions;
    Low-profile interventions;
    Understanding misbehavior
    symptoms

Mnemonic devices, 65, 67 (table)
Motivation
  energetic music as, 43, 97
  intrinsic *vs.* extrinsic motivation
    and, 100–101
  learned helplessness and, 129
  as positive discipline goal, 101
  stress disorder and, 130
Movement of body
  ADD students and, 133
  ADHD students and, 83, 125–126, 133
  body spelling exercises and, 84
  as brain-compatible strategy, 67 (table)
  cerebellum development and, 83
  chronic behavioral conditions and,
    132–133
  classroom applications of, 83–85
  cognitive skills and, 83
  frontal lobe development and, 83
  kinesthetic learners and, 83
  learning enhanced by, 65–66, 83–84
  misbehavior prevention and, 83, 85
  movement and the brain and, 81–82
  music and, 84
  neurotransmitters and, 82
  oxygen to the brain and, 83–84
  phys ed classes, extracurricular
    activities and, 83
  procedural and muscle memory and,
    81–82
  real-life problem solving and, 84
  reflection and application regarding, 86
  review activity and, 84
  role playing and, 66, 82, 84
  stress disorder, depression and, 134
  stretch breaks and, 85
  test scores improvement and, 83
  theoretical framework regarding, 82–83
Muller, C., 19
Muscle memory, 81–82
Music, *42*
  addiction recovery and, 44
  ADHD and, 44
  at-risk behavior and, 44
  as brain-compatible strategy, 67 (table)
  calming the brain for learning and, 10,
    42, 44–45, 54, 132
  celebrating success and, 45, 107
  chronic behavior and, 132
  classical music effects and, 43
  classroom applications of, 44–45
  creating music and, 45
  energizing music and, 45, 97
  feel-good music and, 87
  group energy alignment and, 44
  laughter and, 88
  as memory tool, 41–42, 43
  mood changes and, 10, 42, 43, 44
  motivation and, 43, 97
  movement of students and, 84